HOPE IS A DECISION

HOPE IS A DECISION

SELECTED ESSAYS OF

DAISAKU IKEDA

WITH A FOREWORD BY SARAH WIDER

MIDDLEWAY

P R E S S

Published by Middleway Press
606 Wilshire Blvd., Santa Monica, CA 90401

In association with Dialogue Path Press
Ikeda Center for Peace, Learning, and Dialogue
396 Harvard St., Cambridge, MA 02138

Printed in the United States of America.

Design by Gopa & Ted2, Inc.
ISBN: 978-0-9779245-8-5

Library of Congress Cataloging-in-Publication Data

Names: Ikeda, Daisaku, author.
Title: Hope is a decision : selected essays of Daisaku Ikeda.
Description: Santa Monica, CA : Middleway Press, 2017. |
   Includes bibliographical references and index.
Identifiers: LCCN 2017007065 (print) | LCCN 2017012744 (ebook) |
   ISBN 9781938252693 (ebook pdf) | ISBN 9781938252709 (ePUB) |
   ISBN 9781938252716 (mobi/kindle) | ISBN 9780977924585
   (trade paper : alk. paper)
Subjects: LCSH: Hope--Religious aspects--Buddhism.
Classification: LCC BQ8418.6 (ebook) | LCC BQ8418.6 .I34 2017 (print) |
   DDC 294.3/420428--dc23
LC record available at https://lccn.loc.gov/2017007065

25 24 23 22 21   2 3 4 5 6

TABLE OF CONTENTS

FOREWORD
DECIDING FOR HOPE

WHAT FILLS YOU with hope? I ask that question with urgency, in this time where despair is in the air we breathe. Consider the "moment" in which I write. Violence has seemingly become the default setting in human behavior from the wars that destroy lives in every part of the world to the language we use in everyday life. Consider this small example. When a person succeeds, whether in sports or on an exam or in an assignment at work, how often we hear the phrase "I killed it." In common parlance, success is equated with a violent act. "Just a phrase" is the common response. Would that it were a meaningless metaphor, but in the time it has taken me to write these thoughts (two minutes), in the United States alone, someone has been sexually assaulted. In the world, thirty-four thousand people are rendered homeless each day by the violence that structures the current world.[1]

How do we even talk about hope, let alone participate in it, given the present time? As Daisaku Ikeda notes in his final essay for this collection, the Doomsday Clock stands at 11:55 p.m. We have five minutes left. That essay was written in

2007. Given the continued growth of carbon emissions and the escalation of climate disruption, given the heightened rhetoric of violence that nations adopt and the escalating violence they enact on others, five minutes has dwindled to two and a half. What, then, is the use of hope?

In these essays, written and published over the course of an also tumultuous and violent fifty years, Ikeda calls us to understand hope in a way we may have forgotten or perhaps never known. He asks his readers to learn its range, to listen to its heart, to study its many and varied manifestations. Hope may be as familiar as a friend's encouragement, as near as the tree that grows in an unlikely place, as immediate as the harmonies that come into our thoughts. At the same time, Ikeda reminds us that hope is neither easy nor does it mean acquiescence to injustice. These essays open our eyes to the profound and courageous determination required of those who decide for hope.

Travel with me, if you will, through some of the realities. They may well bring to mind today's world, where bombs rain daily in Aleppo, Syria, where prison, as Henry David Thoreau observed in the late 1840s, becomes the place where the just are kept. Ikeda takes us into his life, into his friends' lives, his mother's life, a brother's death during World War II. In what might be thought of as the emotional center of this collection, he describes the heart-wrenching conversations he shared with a friend when hope threatened to become an empty word ("Children of War"). Since that war, he has dedicated his life to the abolition of nuclear weapons, to the healing of the earth, to creating and supporting peace-centered education, and he has undertaken a particular form of hope-based dialogue with everyone he meets. Through his writing, he brings us into those dialogues, reflecting on what he has learned while thinking together with historian Arnold Toynbee, writers Yoshida Shoin and Oswald Mbuyiseni Mtshali, his mentor, Josei Toda, and so many others.

What humans call death is no barrier to dialogue. Ikeda shows us how words and the actions those words defined and supported live long after they were first written or spoken or taken. The courage, the strength, and the insight of those who lived before us are present with us *if* we realize it. *If* we make real the generosity of spirit and the justice of heart their lives embodied. Here is an ever young Walt Whitman showing a young and potentially despairing Daisaku Ikeda how one could "cast aside all racial prejudices and [break] down all class barriers." Ikeda heard Mahatma Gandhi's call to resist the absolute despair of violence and live the courage of nonviolence. For the readers Ikeda imagines, that, too, is their decision. He invites his readers—he invites us—to take the time we need and the time we must to engage with such courage.

Who are those readers? Each essay was originally published in a particular place at a particular time. They range in date from the mid-1960s to the mid-2000s and speak to the increasing isolation felt in the late twentieth century and today, whether one is a young person seeking a purpose-full life or an elder facing a society that shuns age and fears death. Written from the lived knowledge of Japan during and after World War II, the essays ask readers to consider scrupulously their thoughts, their words, their actions, *and* the consequences of all that they think, say, and do. For as long as Daisaku Ikeda has been writing, as can be seen so beautifully in his early poem "Blossoms that scatter," his words call upon us to engage deeply in what I have come to call "consequential thinking." The wisdom traditions of the world have taught this understanding across time: It is the heart of the Seventh Generation Principle[2] known to have been central to the Haudenosaunee Confederacy and essential to indigenous communities around the world. It is inseparable from Buddhism, with its understanding of co-dependent origination. It resounds in Ubuntu: "I am because we are." The reality of interconnectedness persists across time, not simply time as humans measure it, but *across the deep time of existence.*

Given the profoundly relational world he calls us into, some readers may find Ikeda's emphasis on the individual surprising. In societies created by colonization and industrialization, such emphasis means the oppression of others, now and in the future; it means the exploitation of the land, now and for the future. Ikeda's "individual," however, is not the individual of Western colonialism. Perhaps better termed an "*un*dividual," this person is undivided, inseparable from the profound and intricate interconnectedness that is existence. When Ikeda celebrates every person's agency, he asks us to consider how societal structures have made most human lives dispensable. The few benefit at the expense of most. When Ikeda addresses a person's potential, its fruition depends upon the relations it honors. As he comments, every "individual" shares a common purpose: to "build a society in which people feel valued and fulfilled throughout the course of their lives." Fulfillment is never found in the commodified and consumerized version that trades in fear and despair. He reminds us that we live in a profoundly relational world. To decide for hope, we must think and feel and act within a lived understanding of connectedness and its far-reaching consequences.

Depending upon our cultural backgrounds, our lived experiences, and the daily realities that frame our lives, we may resist or embrace this understanding, term it "naive" or call it home. We may sorrow over how it has been denigrated by other ways of thinking or wonder why it has not been something we have lived from birth. Wherever we live in relation to relatedness, Ikeda speaks to what it means and can mean were we all able to know fully and unabashedly connection with the world around us. Here the English language falls short. Those little words that show direction—*around*, *toward*, *in*, *through*—often separate what is indivisible. The world is not "around" an individual. As Ikeda comments, there is the "vastness of the universe, the eternal flow of time."

In that vastness and flow, Ikeda finds the source and strength of hope: in story related through the poetic spirit. There is nothing more profoundly connective than to be able to listen, truly listen, to another's story—a person's story, the land's story. To share with a good heart one's own story and have that story received with a good heart affirms and continues, even when those stories are wrought with pain. Ikeda reminds us that it is humanly possible to share "the realities of sufferings and challenges" in a healthful and life-affirming way. It need not be condescending or colonizing or controlling. It need not perpetuate the status quo but in fact can be and is the genius of change.

Ikeda calls this genius the "poetic spirit," something that is the birthright of every person. Reclaiming "poetry" from the ephemeral and abstract, Ikeda shows how we all know this as the "heart's unstoppable outpouring." In the essay titled "Each of Us a Poet," he writes, "The poetic spirit can be found in any human endeavor." He includes the work of science, the always ongoing work of social justice, and the everyday work of living without causing harm. He writes:

> The poetic spirit has the power to retune and reconnect a discordant, divided world. True poets stand firm, confronting life's conflicts and complexities. Harm done to anyone, anywhere, causes agony in the poet's heart.

If we do not feel that agony, Ikeda reminds us, we have not yet realized our human potential, we have not yet embodied the poetic spirit, we have not yet decided for hope.

Hamilton, New York   *Sarah Wider*
May 2017   *Professor of English and Women's*
                                  Studies, Colgate University

EDITORS' NOTE

HOPE. For Buddhist thinker Daisaku Ikeda, this is the starting point and endpoint of everything. It is the one thing that makes all the difference in the world.

Ikeda has always put questions of hope front and center in his writing: How do we find hope in dark times that seem to be growing darker? How do we find hope when faced with personal problems that are seemingly impossible to overcome? How do we make a small glimmer of hope grow into a huge sun?

In selecting the essays for this collection, we searched Ikeda's writings for various publications over the last fifty years, intending to answer the question of how Ikeda came to his deep faith in the power of hope. Was he born with it? Did he learn it?

As the autobiographical essays in this volume attest, Ikeda, as a teenager in Japan during World War II, struggled mightily to find a way forward for himself, his family, and his friends. His ardent search for hope eventually led him to his Buddhist teacher, Josei Toda, whom he met at age nineteen, a couple of years after Japan's defeat.

We also wanted this book to show how Ikeda's faith in hope is really a *philosophy* of hope that is completely rooted in Buddhist thought. Another name for this hope is *human revolution*, a term used by Toda that has become a trademark of the international Soka Gakkai Buddhist organization. Human revolution is, however, a concept that anyone, Buddhist or not, can apply and benefit from—the main idea being that hope is found within. And that this hope fully awakened in even one person, then shared with others, can change everything for everyone.

As Ikeda puts it in these pages:

> Working for people's happiness is something everyone can do, regardless of circumstances. It requires no special titles or qualifications. In the end, it simply comes down to engaging with and encouraging others. But this encouragement is not something offered at arm's length, keeping oneself at a safe distance. Real encouragement is conveyed only in sharing the realities of sufferings and challenges.

Ikeda thus argues that true hope can only be found in "sharing the realities of sufferings and challenges" with others. He never pretends that becoming a fully hopeful person is something easy, something that can be quickly accomplished.

He acknowledges that "there may be times when, confronted by cruel reality, we verge on losing all hope. If we cannot feel hope, it is time to create some. We can do this by digging deeper within . . . ."

Everything written by this highly prolific writer circles back to this idea of "digging deeper within." Ikeda's own life has been a triumph of "digging deeper within" for the answers. His philosophy is one of "digging deeper within." And in *Hope Is a Decision*, he encourages the reader to join him in the digging.

HOPE AND HAPPINESS

THE MOST
IMPORTANT DECISION

LOOKING AT THE WORLD today, it is easy to feel despair. A kind of powerlessness seems to be the prevailing mood in the world today. Decisions about important issues all seem to be made somewhere beyond our reach. What can one person accomplish in the face of the vast forces that run our world? The current of the times can seem so fast flowing and complex as to be overwhelming.

I do not believe that people are powerless. The philosophical tradition that I embrace teaches on the most fundamental dimension—that of life itself—that each human life partakes of the limitless life force of the cosmos. The same power that moves the universe exists within our lives. Each individual has immense potential, and a great change in the inner dimension of one individual's life has the power to touch others' lives and transform society. Everything begins with us.

As Nigerian author and poet Ben Okri wrote in his poem "Mental Fight":

You can't remake the world
Without remaking yourself.
Each new era begins within.
It is an inward event,
With unsuspected possibilities
For inner liberation.

The term my mentor, Josei Toda, used for this process of inner transformation that also transforms our surroundings was *human revolution*. And I believe it is the most fundamental, most vital of all revolutions. It can create changes that are more lasting and valuable than political, economic, or technological revolutions. For no matter how external factors change, the world will never get better as long as people remain selfish and apathetic.

An inner change for the better in a single person—one person becoming wiser, stronger, more compassionate—is the essential first turn of the wheel toward realizing peaceful coexistence and fulfillment for the whole human race. I firmly believe that a great human revolution in just one person can be the start of a transformation in the destiny of whole societies and all humankind. And for the individual, everything starts in the inner reaches of life itself.

When we change our inner determination, everything begins to move in a new direction. The moment we make a powerful resolve, every nerve and fiber in our being will immediately orient itself toward the fulfillment of this goal or desire. On the other hand, if we think, "This is never going to work out," then every cell in our body will be deflated and give up the fight.

Hope, in this sense, is a decision. It is the most important decision we can make. Hope changes everything, starting with our lives. Hope is the force that enables us to take action to make our dreams come true. It has the power to change winter into summer, barrenness to creativity, agony to joy. As long as we have hope, there is nothing we cannot achieve. When we possess the treasure of hope, we can draw forth our inner potential and strength. A person of hope can always advance.

Hope is a flame that we nurture within our hearts. It may be sparked by someone else—by the encouraging words of a friend, relative, or mentor—but it must be fanned and kept burning through our own determination. Most crucial is our determination to continue to believe in the limitless dignity and possibilities of both ourselves and others.

Mahatma Gandhi led the nonviolent struggle for Indian independence from British colonial rule, succeeding against all odds. He was, in his own words, an "irrepressible optimist." His hope was not based on circumstances, rising and falling as things seemed to be getting better or worse. Rather, it was based on an unshakable faith in humanity, in the capacity of people for good. He absolutely refused to abandon his faith in his fellow human beings.

Keeping faith in people's essential goodness, and the consistent effort to cultivate this goodness in ourselves: These are the twin keys, as Gandhi proved, to unleashing the great power of hope. Believing in ourselves and in others in this way—continuing to wage the difficult inner struggle to make this the basis for our actions—can transform a society that sometimes seems to be plummeting toward darkness into a humane, enlightened world, where all people are treated with respect.

There may be times when, confronted by cruel reality, we verge on losing all hope. If we cannot feel hope, it is time to create some. We can do this by digging deeper within, searching for even a small glimmer of light, for the possibility of a way to begin to break through the impasse before us.

And our capacity for hope can actually be expanded and strengthened by difficult circumstances. Hope that has not been tested is nothing more than a fragile dream. Hope begins from this challenge, this effort to strive toward an ideal, however distant it may seem.

It is far better to pursue a remote, even seemingly impossible goal than to cheat ourselves of the forward motion that such goals can provide. I believe that the ultimate tragedy in life is not physical death. Rather, it is the spiritual death of losing hope, giving up on our own possibilities for growth.

Toda once wrote:

In looking at great people of the past, we find that they remained undefeated by life's hardships, by life's pounding waves. They held fast to hopes that seemed mere fantastic dreams to other people. They let nothing stop or discourage them from realizing their aspirations. The reason for this, I feel certain, is that their hopes themselves were not directed toward the fulfillment of personal desires or self-interest but based on a wish for all people's happiness, and this filled them with extraordinary conviction and confidence.

Here he pointed to a crucially important truth: Real hope is found in committing ourselves to vast goals and dreams— dreams such as a world without war and violence, a world where everyone can live in dignity.

The problems that face our world are daunting in their depth and complexity. Sometimes, it may be hard to see where—or how—to begin. But we cannot be paralyzed by despair. We must each take action toward the goals we have set and in which we believe. Rather than passively accepting things as they are, we must embark on the challenge of creating a new reality. It is in this effort that true, undying hope is to be found.

—2005

⚆⚆ COURAGE,
⚆⚆ CONVICTION, HOPE

ALL PEOPLE, I suppose, have memories of their youth. Indeed, if they don't, they can hardly be said to have lived their younger years at all. I, like everyone else, have my share.

My family was poor, and my four older brothers were all inducted into the Japanese army and sent off to the front (during World War II). As a result, I had neither the money nor the free time to go to school in the ordinary way. Instead, I worked during the day and, with the money I made, attended business school, and later college, in the evening.

My health was not very good. In spite of that, I tried to do my job the very best I could. There were times when, running errands for the company I worked for, I had to plod through Ginza, Tokyo, pulling a large cart. Other times, I remember having only a single open-collared shirt to wear, even when fall winds began to blow. But I didn't feel any sense of shame or embarrassment. Rather, I saw myself as a figure in a kind of drama—a youth, smiling, battling the hardships of life—and I even felt a sense of pride. As a matter of fact, I'm certain that the hardships I had to undergo at that time helped me to build the foundation for my present way of life.

At that time, I had a certain conviction—no, it would be more accurate to call it a resolution. I believed that youth was not something to be lived in vain. I was determined that, poor and shabby as I might be, I would walk with my head held high, taking whatever encouragement I could find and living life to the fullest. This determination, which gave me great strength, I hold unchanged today. All considerations of position, wealth, and reputation aside, the final victory lies in knowing that you are doing your best as a human being; it is the greatest kind of victory. This is something I intend to never forget until the end of my days.

As I look back over my youth, there are things that give me pause for reflection. For one thing, I wish that in my teens and twenties I had done more studying, particularly in basic subjects. I was certainly aware of how important the period of youth is, and I thought I was reading quite a few books. But now I regret that I didn't read ten or twenty times the number I did. Also, I wish I had done more to train and toughen up my body.

In hindsight, I realize even more how extremely important the period of one's youth really is. Perhaps it would not be too much to say that the whole later course of our lives is determined by the way we pass the years of our youth.

Young people are in the process of building their lives, and for this very reason they are incomplete. They are unknown quantities with limitless possibilities. Young people bring with them the winds of change and reform, and they are the possessors of an enormous, irrepressible vitality. There is little that can equal the greatness of youth. But if young people should neglect to build their lives and instead spend all their time in idle pursuits, or if they should be overly cautious in their goals and allow themselves to become weak and ineffectual, then they are guilty, one might say, of committing spiritual suicide. No course of action could be more shallow and ill-considered.

We must realize that every young person is to some extent fired by the youthful passions coursing through his or her veins. If only firm direction and purpose can be given to these passions, then there is absolutely no doubt that the young can learn to contribute to the welfare of society and to live lives that are truly meaningful.

Too many of the leaders of today, however, although quick enough to criticize the young, seem to give little thought to their own failures and shortcomings. They think only of their own fame and profit, work only for their own glory and advancement, and have no understanding at all of the minds and hearts of the young.

A few years ago I wrote:

> There can be no question that the rise or fall of the nation and the prosperity or decline of the times is in large part determined by the degree of self-awareness that exists on the part of youth and the direction it takes. . . . There is, however, one fact that must never be overlooked, namely, that whatever constructive efforts youth may engage in, they

must invariably be carried out under the inspiration and guidance of the highest ideals and the ablest of leaders. Without such ideals and such leaders, the passion and vitality of youth, regardless of what age one lives in, will be expended in useless activity. And if the young should be induced to follow false ideologies and leaders, then they will advance in the direction of riot and destruction with the force of an angry torrent.

It is the right of each individual to seek out whatever ideals, whatever philosophies, whatever leaders he or she wishes. I am saddened only by the fact that those in political power today seem incapable of offering anything at all to the young. The leaders must, it seems to me, give greater thought and attention to the direction in which they are leading the people.

Based on my own experience, I would say that the qualities most vital to youth are courage, conviction, and hope. Courageous action on the part of the young is the source from which all else is created.

And it is conviction that guides and lends support to courage. Looking at society today, how many countless people do we see who lack conviction? A life devoted solely to flattering others and chiming in with their views is as empty and worthless as foam upon a wave. Conviction knows no faltering or hesitation, no confusion of aims. It grows naturally out of the effort to fulfill one's responsibilities and mission in life.

Finally, a young person who lives a life that is without hope, who feels he or she has no future, is little more than a living corpse. The greatest people of all are those whose youthful years are full of dreams and ideals, and who continue throughout their lives to pursue them.

Young people are the treasures of the nation, the wealth of the age to come. There is no power to compare with the value of this treasure. To do anything that would jeopardize the future of these young people or deprive them of their vigor is equivalent to casting one's treasures into the sea. Those leaders who would actually go a step further and send the young onto the battlefield, where precious lives are lost forever—surely, they deserve to be called the most evil of people.

I have a great fondness for the young; my greatest delight is to watch them grow. The sight of them maturing in an atmosphere of wisdom, peace, and happiness makes my heart leap with joy. It is my present hope that I may spend the rest of my life walking side by side with the young and breathing the air they breathe. If I may live to see them ascend the platform we have built together and soar aloft one by one in the cause of a culture of peace, I will know the fulfillment of my hopes, the attainment of my greatest joy.

—1966

◖◗ TRUTH
◖◗ CLOSE AT HAND

IF I HAD NOT had Toda for my teacher, I would never have amounted to anything. It took me a long time to realize this. While he was still alive, I was completely wrapped up in the struggle for survival, and during the years following his death (in 1958), I have devoted every ounce of my energy to carrying on and enlarging the work he began. As I look back upon all that has happened in the intervening years and consider in an objective manner what the youth he taught have accomplished thus far, I can see that everything has turned out just as he predicted it would on the various occasions when he talked to me and others about our future. He also told us about events to come in the distant future.

My first meeting with Toda took place on a hot summer night in 1947, when I was nineteen. Tokyo, like the rest of Japan, was under the control of the occupation forces. At that time, the entire area south of the Imperial Palace in Tokyo was little more than a burned-out plain. Only here and there in the desolate night could one see dim lights flickering in the little makeshift shacks erected on the ruins or in the air-raid shelters that served as living quarters for many.

My family lived in the area and made a living by growing and gathering edible seaweed known as nori. We somehow managed to keep the business going during the war and in the years following it, though on a much reduced scale.

In the midst of poverty and want, Japanese society was undergoing profound changes. The cry of democracy was heard on every street corner; the old powers and figures of authority one after another faltered and crumbled.

For my generation, which had nationalism and absolute obedience to the emperor drummed into us from the time we were old enough to understand anything, it seemed as though everything we had believed had suddenly been reduced to naught. We had nothing whatsoever to trust and believe in. It is hardly surprising that we found our bodies and minds tormented day after day by distress and apprehension.

It was under such conditions that, almost as a natural impulse, two or three of us got together in a group to exchange books. Starved for something to read, we treasured whatever volumes we could find that had escaped being burned in the air raids and fell on them hungrily. Novels, works of philosophy, biographies of the great, books on science—we devoured anything and everything that came to hand and then shared our impressions with one another. Although we would have endless debates on the significance of what we had read, when we faced the harsh realities of the times, the spiritual support and confidence we thought we had gained from our reading would suddenly melt away.

In addition to this group, I had another friend from elementary school days who from time to time came to visit me. One day, she invited me to attend a meeting, to be held at her house, on "The Philosophy of Life." It was then that I first heard the name Josei Toda. Purely out of curiosity, I decided to go and took along with me the other members of the reading group.

We found ourselves being addressed by a man in his forties with a somewhat hoarse voice and relaxed manner. His thick glasses caught the light, and I remember being particularly impressed by his broad, prominent forehead. At first, I didn't understand anything he was saying, though I gathered it had to do with Buddhist doctrine. I had no sooner come to that conclusion than I noticed that his remarks were interspersed with acute observations on the political situation and other matters pertaining to everyday life. But just as I would begin to follow what he was saying, he would suddenly come out with a string of difficult-sounding Buddhist terms. In all, my impression was that of a very strange and unfamiliar philosophy.

Still, it did not sound like the usual sermon of a religious leader, nor, for that matter, what one would call a conventional philosophy lecture. It seemed to be concrete and to the point, without any bandying about of abstract ideas and concepts. At the same time, it seemed to suggest that the plain facts of everyday life were in themselves capable of embodying the highest kinds of truth.

The room was filled to overflowing with middle-aged men, housewives, young girls, sturdy-looking young men. All of them kept their eyes fixed on Toda and listened with rapt attention. Though all were shabbily dressed, I knew that they were good, law-abiding people. There seemed to be about these simple people an unexplainable vitality.

Toda did not strike me as belonging to any type of personality that I was familiar with. He had a brusque way of speaking but also conveyed unlimited warmth. As I stared intently at him, our lines of vision would sometimes meet. At such times, I would drop my eyes in confusion, but when I would look up again after a moment, I felt as though his gaze were still fixed upon me. It sounds like an odd thing to say, but in the course of the talk, I somehow began to feel I had known him for a long time.

At the end of the talk, my friend introduced me to Toda. "Well, well," he said, his eyes shining behind the thick lenses as he looked for a moment squarely into my eyes. Then, as though he understood something, he broke into a warm smile.

"How old are you now?" he asked.

With that sense of having known him before, I answered without hesitation, "Nineteen."

"Nineteen, you say?" He seemed to have remembered something. "I was nineteen when I came to Tokyo. I came from Hokkaido, a country hick on my first visit to the big city."

He was chewing on a Jintan tablet, a kind of breath freshener, and smoking a cigarette at the same time. I felt an impulse to take the opportunity to ask him about some of the doubts I had concerning life and society: What is the right kind of life? What does true patriotism mean? What do you think of the emperor system? What is Buddhism really all about?

I did ask him, and his replies were direct and unequivocal. He appeared to be answering without the slightest difficulty, but I now know that that was simply an indication of how rapidly his mind worked. Without any trace of awkwardness or evasion, he addressed himself directly to the heart of each question. I came away fully satisfied with his answers, realizing for the first time in my life that truth was after all something very close at hand.

On August 24, just ten days after that evening, I joined the Soka Gakkai, the Buddhist organization Toda was leading. Little by little, I came to understand the validity of Buddhist philosophy and to appreciate the rarity of a person like Toda.

Meanwhile, I continued to work during the day and go to school in the evenings. But I was unsure about my future, and about a year later, following what seemed to be the most natural course of events, I made up my mind to quit my job and go to work for the publishing company that Toda headed.

That was in January 1949. It was very hard work. The postwar Japanese economy, just recovering from the effects of defeat, was tossed about like a boat on the surging waves of inflation. A modest enterprise like Toda's could not escape being buffeted and battered in the harsh economic climate. From the end of 1949 until the summer of 1951, we fought a battle for survival every day.

One by one, the employees left and went elsewhere, until I was the only person remaining to deal with our creditors. The deterioration of my health and my general frustrations with things not going as I wanted had both reached the crisis point, yet I made no move to leave Toda. On the contrary, I at some point made up my mind that I would stick with him regardless of what happened, even if it meant following him to the depths of hell. I believed in him, I believed in the rightness of the Buddhist teachings, and I was determined to continue the fight as long as possible.

"I have failed in business, but I have not failed in my life, and I have not failed in Buddhism!" In uttering these words, Toda showed me that he was fully aware of his mission. This was something I sensed strongly. From that point onward, everything was a matter of rebuilding.

To help Toda rebuild his business and the Soka Gakkai, which had been decimated during the war, it became necessary for me to give up my schooling. Toda was sorry that, as his only disciple, I had to take this step. "From now on," he said, "I'll teach you everything!"

For the next several years, I received private instruction from Toda at his home or early in the morning at his office. Law, political science, economics, chemistry, astronomy, the Chinese classics—with the utmost care, he taught me almost every conceivable subject, except foreign languages. It seemed as though he were determined to pass on to me every bit of learning that he himself possessed.

He was largely self-educated. After finishing elementary school in Hokkaido, he became an apprentice to a tradesman, simultaneously studying on his own until he qualified himself as an assistant elementary school teacher. He then took a job as a teacher in a coal-mining region in Yubari and in time became a regular teacher. At nineteen he came to Tokyo, where he happened to become acquainted with Tsunesaburo Makiguchi, the man who was to be his teacher for the rest of Makiguchi's life. He attended middle school classes at night and eventually passed the examination certifying that he had completed the equivalent of four years of middle school training.[3] Later, he studied at Chuo University. Being largely self-educated, he needed schools not to acquire learning but to give certification to the learning he had already gained.

He was especially versed in mathematics and for a time operated a successful private tutorial school, called the Jishu Gakkan. Also, under the pen name Jogai Toda, he wrote a book titled *Guide to Arithmetic*, which was much used by students reviewing for exams and which sold more than a million copies, making it one of the bestsellers of the time. Many who were students in those days remember the book with fondness.

In addition to the various subjects I already mentioned, Toda gave me instruction, and this with great intensity and enthusiasm, in the life philosophy of Buddhism. As he passed on to me detailed explanations of the Buddhist teachings, he drew my attention to the ways in which these teachings related to various kinds of modern thought. I have subsequently come to realize that, in addition to this formal instruction, his efforts to rebuild the Soka Gakkai, and in fact every aspect of his daily life, were a form of teaching, earnestly shared and of inestimable value.

I responded to this intense, challenging training with the best I could muster in diligence and endurance. I tried to absorb everything he had to give me, though I fell short of his expectations so often that, almost until the day of his death, I was subject to frequent scoldings.

Reflecting on my life leaves me awestruck at just how much Toda's existence has meant to me. That a man so mediocre as myself could succeed Toda as head of the Soka Gakkai and assist in the unprecedented undertaking of widely sharing the spirit and teachings of Buddhism is due solely to the fact that I have never for so much as an instant let the image of this great leader leave my mind and heart. The greatest happiness of my life is that I met him and became his disciple, and that this relationship between us of teacher and student lasted until the end of his life.

—1969

◖◗ WINTER
◖◗ NEVER LASTS

ON THE LONG VOYAGE of life, there are times when the sun shines with the warmth and brightness of a spring day. There are other times, like bitter winter nights, when we must battle the freezing cold. Periods of hardship, we might say, are the winter nights of life.

Some people encounter their worst hardships during their youth and then, having successfully overcome them, go on to live in relative ease and happiness for the rest of their days. There are others who succeed in avoiding hardship during their youth only to have it descend upon them in old age.

In my case, I tried to experience what hardships I could in my youth, hoping that in the process of overcoming them I could build a firm foundation for later life. Not that I had the slightest intention of going out of my way to invite unusual hardship or to be anything more than an ordinary human being. In fact, I realize that there are untold numbers who have struggled, and continue to struggle, against far greater difficulties than I have.

But because I had my share of sickness and poverty and

other such worries, I can now in full measure sympathize with others who are sick or troubled. It is something I am deeply thankful for.

Walt Whitman's spirit was that the more one has shivered in the cold, the better one can appreciate the warmth of the sun; the more troubles one has experienced in the world, the better one can understand the true value of human life. Indeed, winter never lasts forever. After the bitter struggles of winter is bound to come the sunshine of spring.

The important thing is never to give in to hardship. In times of trial, one must learn to endure whatever may come and thereby strengthen and improve oneself. After all, it is only the person who has experienced the cold of winter who can savor and enjoy with one's whole being the warm sunshine of spring.

"The star that governs your destiny is in your own heart," another poet has said. There can be no doubt about it. Whatever one's circumstances, whatever one's past, the star of destiny, the forces that determine one's future, are nowhere but in one's own heart and mind.

Regardless of what storms may blow, what angry waves may threaten, you must keep shining at all times with a pure, steady light. This is what I want to say to all the young people of today who are undergoing hardship, for depending on how you bear up under that hardship, the trials of today could turn out to be your most precious possessions.

As I have mentioned elsewhere, I had four elder brothers. Since all four were called into military service during World War II, I was left with many of the tasks and responsibilities that under ordinary circumstances would have been theirs. Our house was burned down in the air raids, and though my parents both worked as hard as they could and tried not to burden their children, I naturally had to look out to some extent for my younger brothers and my little sister.

Moreover, I was at that time suffering from tuberculosis, and much of my strength was consumed simply in battling the disease. In any ordinary Japanese family today, a person in the condition I was in would as a matter of course be sent to a sanatorium for an extended period of treatment and rest. But in the years I am speaking about, toward the end of the war and just after it, such a step was out of the question.

Every day was a struggle for me. Toward evening, the low fever symptomatic of the disease would invariably come on. Then, there was the cough, which never let up. How many times, even after I had gone to bed, it persisted, tormenting me so that I could hardly get to sleep.

The doctor at one point said I would probably not last much past twenty-three or twenty-four. After I went to work at Toda's company, my health continued to be a constant source of worry for him, and he on one occasion confided to my parents that he did not think I would live to see thirty. But I kept on day after day doing the best I could to carry out my job, strenuous though it was. I don't mean by this to sound as though I am advising people to do anything foolish or to deliberately put an undue strain on their health. But as I look back at my own case, I have a feeling that if I hadn't had the daily challenge of my job before me, my body might well have succumbed to the disease. Because I knew that I had a job to do, both my body and my spirit rose to the challenge. Eventually, I regained my health.

As Miguel de Cervantes wrote in *Don Quixote*, "While there's life there's hope."[4] There were many times when my condition was so bad that I lost all courage and was on the point of resigning myself to death. But I would say to myself, "I'm still alive, which means there is still hope!" I would resolve to go on fighting.

I know there must be any number of people in the world today much sicker than I ever was. I would appeal to such people to face their trials with a firm, undespairing heart and to never surrender in their battle with disease. And this applies not only to disease: No matter what kind of difficult situations one finds oneself in, some opportunity, some opening, can always be found to fight one's way out. The important thing is always to have hope and to face the future bravely.

I went to work for Toda in January 1949, when I was twenty-one. My job was editing a magazine, and for someone in my physical condition, it was hard work. But, as I have already said, the fact that I had the work to challenge me each day turned out in fact to be a blessing.

I was also receiving intensive instruction and training from Toda in a number of different subjects. Sometimes, I would find myself being scolded by him with a fury like that of a hundred thunderbolts striking all at once, while at other times he would show me infinite gentleness and patience. I never had the slightest doubt that at heart he had deep faith in me and that behind the scolding was his loving concern and desire to make me into a person of real worth, capable of doing any kind of work. For this reason, it was a boundless joy to work for him, and I never for a moment thought of giving up.

A truly warm human relationship—how much in the way of hope and courage and conviction it is capable of giving! It is not too much to say that, in the end, everything I have today I owe to the fact that I encountered such a great teacher, one who was willing to trust me without question. To be looked upon as trustworthy and reliable is surely one of the most valuable assets a person can have, regardless of occupation. And for a young person, to be trusted at work is of prime importance. If a young person does not learn to inspire trust in others, failure is almost certain.

At present, they say, we are living in an age of irresponsibility. There is a tendency for people to not only disregard but to be completely indifferent to the trust that others put in them. But so long as human society exists, it is patent that trustworthiness will continue to be of basic importance. Anyone who betrays this trust will become a social outcast, eventually having to taste the bitterness of defeat. Today, one may smugly flaunt an irresponsible manner; in the end, nothing but grief will result.

I believe it was the Japanese novelist Saneatsu Mushanokoji who said, "One word from a person who is qualified to be trusted carries more weight than ten thousand words from someone who is not." Trust is hard to build up and easy to destroy. Trust that one has spent ten years in nurturing can be wiped out in an instant by some little slip-up in word or action.

A pretentious, overconfident manner that tries to hide one's lack of real ability will quickly be exposed when a time of crisis arises. Those who work with all their might to carry out their mission will in the end win the trust of those around them. The type of person I most respect is one who, though he or she may be doing a rather inconspicuous, unexciting job, still does it conscientiously, advancing step by step and patiently working toward self-improvement.

When I speak of the importance of inspiring trust, I certainly do not mean that one should be constantly choosing the safest course and trying to succeed at all costs. For a young person, this is a fatal error. On the contrary, the mistakes of one's youth are often far more important than we could ever guess in helping to build one's foundation for the future. Therefore, I hope to see young people do each day's work with courage, aware that they still have much to learn but determined to do their best. The Irish novelist Oliver Goldsmith wrote, "Our greatest glory is, not in never falling, but in rising every time we fall."[5]

I have forgotten the author, but the following words also come to mind, words that have always moved me deeply:

> Failure—what is failure? Is it not a constant occurrence in the world? And is it not the ladder to great accomplishment? Because of it, we gain a kind of experience that we could never acquire from ten thousand books. . . . Ah! Failure is the means by which Heaven bestows happiness upon us. In truth, it is the greatest treasure of life!

To lose heart just because of one or two failures is the height of foolishness. Life is a long, long journey. No matter how wonderful a life you have lived, if you in the end find yourself defeated and unhappy, nothing could be more miserable.

In youth, one should go forward with courage, understanding that the more often one fails, the firmer will be the foundation for one's future life and happiness.

It is also necessary for young people to have the fearlessness to recognize their failures as failures and honestly take responsibility for them. This kind of attitude I find most admirable in young people. Above all, one must avoid the opposite tendency, refusing to recognize one's responsibility and like a coward trying to shift the blame to others.

Finally, one must have the breadth of mind to consider the source of one's failures and in a cool, objective manner to judge how and where one went wrong. For such judgment will serve as the source of future value.

The sight of a young person striving to reach the goal he or she has set is one of the most powerful, most refreshing, most beautiful things in the world. Nowhere in the world is there a beauty to match that of a young person who has fought with and overcome hardship.

—1967

⚉ ⚉ TOO MUCH
⚉ ⚉ STRESS

W E **LIVE IN** a high-pressure, high-stress society. In Japan, the symptoms of extreme levels of stress are seen in the "death from overwork" syndrome and a tragically high suicide rate. Vicious bullying among children is likewise a reflection of this stress.

Martin Seligman, renowned for his research into the psychology of hope, expresses his concern about what he calls "big I and small we"—a distended self-centeredness and an increasingly attenuated sense of connection with others. It seems clear this trend must be confronted if we are to prevent our lives from growing even more stressful.

In the past, human society provided encouragement and opportunity for people to extend support to one another, especially in highly stressful situations. Regrettably, many of the networks that supported us have been weakened or undermined. Faced with stress, too many people feel they have nowhere to turn, that they don't have access to the kind of friendships or communities where they can easily, openly share their problems and worries.

The term *stress* is originally from physics and refers to the deformation of a body that has been subjected to external forces. It later came to be used to refer to the effect of various pressures on the mental and physical well-being of people.

Needless to say, just as different materials bear up better or worse under the strain of physical pressure, the ability to deal with stressful situations varies widely from person to person. A work or interpersonal situation that one individual finds intolerably stressful might, for someone else, not even register as stress. The same person will also be affected by stress differently on different occasions. Even seemingly happy events such as marriage or a job promotion will often provoke a stress reaction.

For this reason, telling someone that their problem is no big deal, even with the helpful intention of encouraging them, might actually deepen and intensify their experience of stress. The reactions of the human heart are not mechanical and predictable but infinitely subtle and delicate.

From one perspective, core sources of stress can be traced to our contemporary ideas about the nature of the self. On the one hand, we are each expected, as "free individuals," to be able to deal unaided with any situation. And at the same time, the massive bureaucratic structures of society treat us as components and cogs, inculcating the sense that we are powerless to shape our fate, much less to move human society in a new, better direction. Torn between excessive expectations and feelings of ultimate powerlessness, we can become increasingly susceptible to the impact of stress.

Coping successfully with stress requires that we try to see ourselves in a different light. We need a deeper understanding of our limitless potential as well as our vulnerabilities, how we can develop our strengths as individuals through mutual support.

Hans Selye, a pioneer in the field of stress research, offered the following advice based on his own experience of battling cancer: First, establish and maintain your own goals in life. Second, live so that you are necessary to others—such a way of life is ultimately beneficial to yourself.

It is natural for us, as human beings, to look forward. Our eyes naturally look ahead. In this sense, we are made for moving toward a goal. At the same time, reaching out to others who suffer strengthens our ability to meet our own problems and challenges with courage.

The Buddhist sutras contain this well-known parable: One day, Shakyamuni Buddha was approached by a woman wracked by grief at the loss of her child. She begged him to bring her baby back to life. Shakyamuni comforted her and offered to prepare medicine that would revive her child. To make this, he would need a mustard seed, he said, which he instructed her to find in a nearby village. This mustard seed, however, would have to come from a home that had never experienced the death of a family member.

The woman set out from house to house, asking each family for a mustard seed. But nowhere could she find a home that had never known death. As she continued her quest, the woman accepted that her child had died and began to realize her suffering was something shared by all people. She returned to Shakyamuni determined not to be overwhelmed by grief.

Physical and intellectual training transform our experiences. The same steep slope that for the unskilled skier provokes only terror is, for the expert, a source of excitement and joy. Likewise, with persistent study, we can draw knowledge and inspiration from the deepest, most difficult text. Just as physical training can bring forth the unseen capacities of our bodies and intellectual training develops our minds, our hearts can be trained and strengthened.

Through the process of overcoming grief, for example, it becomes possible for us to see beyond our own sufferings and concerns to develop a more expansive, robust sense of self. This experience can inspire our compassionate acts for others who have known this same pain.

By working with and for the sake of others, it is possible to make even stressful situations an opportunity to learn to live with enhanced energy and focus. It seems unlikely that the sources of stress we face will decrease; it seems highly probable that they will increase. Now, more than ever, we need to develop the qualities of strength, wisdom, and hope as we build networks of mutual support.

In the end, the key to living in a stress-filled society lies in feeling the suffering of others as our own—in unleashing the universal human capacity for empathy. There is no need for anyone to carry the burden of a heavy heart alone.

—2006

FRIENDSHIP AND POETRY

⚬⚬ TRUE
⚬⚬ FRIENDS

I **AM A SO-CALLED** "child of Edo"—a native of Tokyo. As such I tend to be simple, straightforward, and trusting by nature and therefore easily taken advantage of by others. My mentor often consoled me on this account, saying that it is better to be deceived by others than to deceive. But he also offered me guidance, saying that unless I learned to keenly discern the character of the person I was working with, I could never become a great leader.

To really know another person is fairly difficult. In most cases, you cannot judge someone by appearances alone. Even if you think you understand a person, you might be surprised at the depth they display when the occasion calls for it. It's difficult to gauge someone through a brief encounter, especially when it comes to their core nature.

Friendship is nurtured through deliberate, repeated engagement, which will give rise to deep understanding and the cultivation of each other's character.

This being so, it might also be said that a person's character is revealed in what kind of friends they have. An ancient sage also stresses the importance of having wise teachers and good friends, saying: "If you wish to know a person, take a look at his friends. If you wish to know a ruler, look at those who stand beside him." As these words suggest, a person with an attractive character gathers excellent friends just as a magnet attracts iron. Through mutual interaction and encouragement, friends can help one another improve.

Nichiren, the thirteenth-century Buddhist reformer whose teachings the Soka Gakkai embraces, also comments on friendship: "You have associated with a friend in the orchid room and have become as straight as mugwort growing among hemp."[6] "A friend in the orchid room" indicates a person of high virtue, and "as straight as mugwort growing among hemp" suggests the development of a good, upright character.

Indeed, association with genuine good friends is the fertile soil from which the rich, abundant fruits of life will grow.

In one of the sutras, Shakyamuni likens a good friend to the sun rising on the horizon:

> Monks, all of you are aware of the way the sun rises in the morning. Prior to the sunrise, the eastern skies begin to glow. Then a huge flaming light emerges and soon the sun begins to rise. In other words, the brilliant eastern skies signal the sunrise's imminent appearance. In the same vein, when you monks aspire to the noble eightfold path, there are also certain omens. They are the possession of good friends. Those of you who have good friends will,

with certainty, master the noble eightfold path and
acquire virtuous attributes.

I think this is a beautiful, apt analogy. On several occasions,
I have observed the sunrise in India. I was moved in particular
when I thought of Shakyamuni a few thousand years before,
preaching the truth to his disciples while viewing the same
sunrise.

Shakyamuni was said to possess "teacherless wisdom"; he
attained the wisdom of a Buddha without the aid of a teacher.
This enlightened man, however, must have had thorough
insight into the nature of human weakness: that left to their
own devices, people will find it difficult to persevere on the
correct path, let alone attain enlightenment. This is why we
need wise teachers and good friends who at times use strict
words to cultivate our growth, while at other times, offer us
the warm sunshine of encouragement.

Only when embraced by such good people is it possible
for a person to achieve satisfaction in life. One's life will then
be like the sun that continues to shine brilliantly from above,
overflowing with smiles.

Bonds of friendship differ from relationships among family
members or among neighbors. Unlike blood relationships or
those based on geographical proximity, which are, in a sense,
predetermined, friendship is something you deliberately pursue and work to cultivate. Without continual effort to do both,
the friendship will eventually erode and ultimately fade away.

And yet a firm, beautiful friendship can transcend differ-
ences of ethnicity and nationality.

In this sense, I feel that the friendships we maintain serve as a clear mirror that most vividly reflects the depth, independence, and creativity of our way of life. A renowned author once said, "A true friend never misunderstands you, no matter what you say."

In the course of a longstanding acquaintance, mistrust may sometimes naturally arise. Trust, however, is not something you demand first from others.

As you maintain deep faith in the fundamental humanity of others, you will, in due course, acquire true, lasting friendships.

Buddhism places fundamental emphasis on faith. Even Shariputra, known as the wisest of Shakyamuni's disciples, attained enlightenment only through faith. Shakyamuni constantly urged his disciples to associate with good friends in order to cultivate faith, and his emphasis seems to me that of a person of great perception and wisdom who had a complete grasp of the inherent strengths and weaknesses of the human being.

—1980

○○ CHILDREN
○○ OF WAR

FOR THE FIRST TIME in a long while, I've written a letter to a good friend from my elementary school days. When we were in school together, the Sino-Japanese War had already started, and the fires of war were spreading year after year. Everyone was poor.

Childhood is usually a time of imagination and excitement, but the war had driven our country into such a state of misery and desperation that our hearts were unable to soar free and find refuge. We sensed some black, dire event approaching like a storm.

It was an age of unending sorrow and pain. Even if we dreamed, on wings of imagination, of an enjoyable, fairy-tale world, we'd be awakened at dawn by the shrill blast of a military bugle. Parents were torn from their children. And children were torn from their parents and dragged to the battlefield.

From the spring of 1942—shortly after the start of the Pacific War and after finishing my studies at the national people's school[7]—I was forced [at age fourteen] to spend the days of my youth working at the Niigata Steelworks in the neighborhood I grew up in, Kamata, Tokyo.

It wasn't long before the war quickly took a turn for the worse.

My good friend from elementary school used to regularly express his discontent and sorrow to me.

"Aren't our souls allowed to be free?" he asked. "It's just so oppressive always being forced to control our thoughts and feelings. I get so sick of it. The blue sky stretches above us, and flowers bloom in the field, but we are like prisoners. We have nothing to be proud or excited about, nothing to hope for. We are drowning in despair."

The faces of people in the street told the same story; hardly anyone smiled.

One day, we ran into a group of factory workers causing a commotion. They were venting their pent-up frustrations at the world by shouting and cursing and generally being rowdy.

"Let's get out of here," said my friend, having no time for such displays. He was the kind of young man who would say, "I just have a stitch in my side," rather than whine, "I'm hungry."

We walked along the nearby Morigasaki Beach. With a thoughtful expression, my friend talked to me seriously for a long time.

"I hate our country," he said. "Japan is truly frightening. Someday, I want to go to Europe. I am prepared to swim, to ride the sea wind, to get out of here and to another country."

The streets were dark at night because of the threat of air raids. There was no food, no clothing. People's homes had been destroyed, and they had nowhere to live. They spoke in hushed, subdued voices. And the sight of people sadly evacuating the city was heartrending.

"I want to be saved by something," said my friend. "If I go on like this, I will become a dead person. There are no bright possibilities to look forward to. There is no future. We're supposed to be entering the best days of our youth, but the road ahead is shrouded in darkness, and I can't see a thing.

"I want to beat a drum and shout something. But day after day is dark and gloomy, and I feel like I'm falling into a world of emptiness and meaninglessness. When I think of my country, which is all in a frenzy over this war, I feel nothing. I wonder if it's just that I am a weak person.

"If people want to abuse me, they can go ahead. If they say I'm frivolous or don't show proper commitment to the cause, let them. But I want to create something solid and enduring, forge an unshakable spirit and inner strength, so that dear friends like you will understand my heart, even after I'm gone.

"My life is my greatest treasure. How can I live my life, so that it will one day shine with glorious triumph? How can I challenge and conquer the humiliations, the cruelties, and the temptations I meet along the way, while always keeping a spirit of indignation toward such things blazing in my heart?

"Right now, I see nothing bright before me. All I see before me is a muddy path with none of the warmth of a nice, thick rug.

"How will these insane times toy with my life? I am exhausted by all the monstrous changes society has gone through, yet I feel sure that the eternal, true reality that I long for and thirst for from the depths of my being lies beyond these dark storm clouds.

"I have begun to deeply ponder the mystery of the human spirit and the treasure that is the life of the universe. There must exist the power to survive even the most calamitous flood. I want to experience for myself the reality of that shining power.

"No matter how foul a road we must traverse, no matter how painful and even bloody the path, I want to keep pressing onward toward the green fields abloom with flowers that lie beyond the present darkness and confusion."

Hot tears fell from my friend's eyes.

A wind was blowing, tapping at the windows of the houses. Our conversation continued. We noted that many people had become spiritually lazy. They didn't have the means to open the window of their mind and see clearly.

But it was blatantly apparent that the hearts of Japan's leaders were putrid. And the great hopes that the people had so long lost sight of were reemerging as a powerful cry and beginning to take shape as a broad popular alliance.

Hope would come; not to be outdone, so would despair. We agreed that the strength to transform even despair into hope had to exist and acknowledged the need, therefore, to forge the inner strength to live true to ourselves, undefeated by disappointment. And we pondered where we could find a philosophy and a mentor that would teach us how to do just that.

Recalling this conversation of many decades ago, I wrote to my old friend. Many of our classmates died in the war. I lost contact with many more in the long chaotic years during and after the war. But I remember them, just as they were when young. They are my precious friends from my hometown, their images engraved deep in my heart.

Mikhail Gorbachev, who is around the same age as I, once said to me that our generation could be described as the "children of war." It certainly is true that as children, we were forced to endure the pain and misery of wars started by our elders. This is precisely why we must never allow future generations of children to experience such cruel tragedy. We must open the way to a century without war, a century of peace. This, I believe, is our destiny and our mission.

—2000

○○ CEMETERY
○○ DAYS

AS JAPAN'S DEFEAT in World War II neared, the people were spiritually desolate and materially bereft. My superior at the Niigata Steelworks showed concern for my health, moving me out of the plant and into the business office. My solitary joy in those days was getting immersed in some book during the noon hour on a strip of grass within the factory compound. I loved to read.

Looking for a quiet place on my day off, I often went to a nearby cemetery and spent the whole day with my face in a book. People rarely visited such a place, so I could concentrate on ambling through my book with no distractions.

I now find my memory no longer as good as it once was, but in my "cemetery days," I was so fascinated by what I read that my mind soaked up everything it touched. I especially liked poetry.

In fact, I committed to memory passages that struck my fancy, even if they were several pages long. I recited them to myself as I walked along the street. For the likes of a person like me, a boy forced to spend his sensitive adolescent days in the shadow of war, books were my best friends. They cheered me up and lent me encouragement.

The war, of course, went badly for Japan. In March 1944, the government established rules for mobilizing middle school students into the workforce. The official announcement of an ordinance for students to be impressed as workers and another that provided for female volunteers came that August. Students from the nearby Ebara Middle School had been mobilized to work in my factory too. Partly because I was around the same age, I got along well with them. Some of my work breaks were spent with five or six friends from that school who shared my interests; we had only a mere ten to twenty minutes, but it was a joy talking with them two or three times a week about literature.

One of these friends was in charge of a backroom used to store blueprints and the like. Our impromptu reading group was lucky enough to be permitted to use that quiet little room for a time and to talk together behind a locked door about books we had recently read. We also cooperated in securing the books we wanted to read, some of us combing second-hand bookstores, others going round to relatives' homes to see if they owned a copy.

"Life is vital!" A friend from the group later told me that this idea was uppermost in my mind at the time. Second was the question "What will the war do to us?"

Probably, my thoughts stemmed from working in a munitions factory, from my experiences of air raids, from my reading, and from the fact that my brothers had been drafted into the army one by one and sent off to war. I'm sure that I was also concerned about the general problem of life itself, for indeed I couldn't help noticing that people close to me were being killed on the battlefields and that my physical infirmities had been adversely affected by the lack of proper nutrition and the like.

By the spring of 1945, American planes attacked Tokyo almost daily. We were drenched with incendiary bombs. The burned-out area to the south of Tokyo kept expanding. Air-raid shelters, the bucket brigade, sirens . . . the victims of the war could not be numbered.

War is incredibly cruel. Even the huge cherry tree that had bloomed in the spacious yard of my boyhood home had been cut down before I knew it, and the yard later became part of a munitions factory. Almost all the homes and factories in neighborhoods that underwent saturation bombing were burned to the ground.

Oddly enough, one corner of a serene Buddhist temple nearby had survived the flames. One day, I was walking alone lost in thought when I noticed that a number of cherry trees in the compound had managed to survive. They were blooming beautifully, full of fragrance. I stopped in my tracks, deeply touched.

I fashioned my feelings at that moment into a poem. Let me share it with you as evidence of one distinct phase in a teenager's life:

Cherries in bloom that the air raid spared
blue sky above them   fallen petals jumbled

for a background the gutted ruins of reality
and the pitiful people who cannot look up to them

bitter are their long wanderings
the road of parent and child

amid the waves of little shacks, flowers in bloom
cherry blossoms—is theirs the hue of dawn?

Ah, there is a simile in this existence
men of power and men of peace

"blossoms that scatter, blossoms that remain
to become blossoms that scatter"—so sings a man

blossoms of youth, how many million—
why must they scatter? why must they scatter?

In distant southern seas, ill-fated cherries
full bloom not yet on them, their branches are
      in pain

and my friends remaining, their hearts, before
      we know it,
wounded by the loss of the world of the ideal

Are all things impermanent? are they eternal?
without even knowing, must we scatter?

Blossoms that scatter, blossoms that remain,
bloom forever, in spring send out your fragrance on
   the storm![8]

I titled this poem, written in the spring the year the war was to end (when I was seventeen), "Blossoms that scatter."

—1975

○○ AN UNFORGETTABLE
○○ BOOK

LEAVES OF GRASS—the title itself suggests vigor and irrepressible growth. Indeed, the book that bears it overflows with youth, hope, the beauty of nature, and the language of equality.

When I look at my copy, I see that it was published on May 31, 1949, the translation done by Saika Tomita. I was twenty-one in 1949, but I remember that I was around twenty-three when I bought the book at a bookstore in Kanda, Tokyo, so I must not have purchased it when it first came out. A watercolor of a branch of flowering acacia graced the attractive dust jacket. It is a thick book—505 pages, I see now.

Most of the books at that time were printed on wretched paper, but this was an exception. Printed on high-class paper, it was a grand, imposing example of bookmaking, especially for that period. I also remember the price, 550 yen, and how worried I was about spending so much money. A book like that today would probably cost thousands of yen.

What a delicious shock lay in store for me! I remember how

profoundly impressed I was by the first poem, a declaration of "modern man" titled "One's-Self I Sing":

> *One's-Self I sing, a simple separate person,*
> *Yet utter the word Democratic, the word En-Masse.*
>
> *Of physiology from top to toe I sing,*
> *Not physiognomy alone nor brain alone is worthy for the*
> *Muse, I say the Form complete is worthier far,*
> *The Female equally with the Male I sing.*[9]

To me, it seemed a hymn to life itself. There were no ghosts of the past here. The poet's eyes were fixed solely upon the glorious vistas unfolding as the present gave way to the future. It was a prophecy of the birth of a new world, the world of America, and of the coming of a new century. And it was a clear farewell to the old world, the stolid, weighty world of European civilization.

Whitman cast aside all racial prejudices and broke down all class barriers. He hated everything in this world that stifles and cramps, singing the praises of all who sweat and labor to build the future.

Before all else, he sang of himself. The long poem titled "Song of Myself," with which the 1855 edition opened, is an example:

> *I celebrate myself, and sing myself,*
> *And what I assume you shall assume,*

For every atom belonging to me as good belongs
  to you.[10]

Around the middle of this long poem, we find this vivid portrait of the poet:

Walt Whitman, a kosmos, of Manhattan the son,
Turbulent, fleshy, sensual, eating, drinking and breeding,
No sentimentalist, no stander above men and women or
    apart from them,
No more modest than immodest.[11]

The poet sang of all the countless beings of the new world, describing them just as they appeared to him in the midst of their comings and goings. How busy it kept him, being the poet of the new world! He could not rest until he had sung of the mountains, the rivers, the seas, even the remote corners of the wilderness and of the city. He sang of all human beings, whether young or old, man or woman, of the farmer, the miner, the laborer, the sailor, the slave, the prostitute, even the assassinated president. He sang of the frustrated revolutionary, the struggling pioneer and the wounded soldier, the wife who had lost a husband, the mother who had lost a son, striving to comfort them all and give them courage. He went on to sing of inanimate things: the ship, the machine, the skyscraper.

He was a man of the universe who, believing firmly in the impulse of simple, unclouded love, sang with all his heart in nineteenth-century America for freedom and equality to reach all, and he went on singing until his death.

In the years following Japan's defeat, when the country was under the occupation forces, I remember with fondness and gratitude what it meant to me, a poor young man, to encounter this collection. When, in the midst of those gray, troubled times, I learned from this book the secret of how to face the future, my initial admiration gave way to an intense affection.

I memorized a number of my particular favorites, and when I was on my way home late at night or at other times, I would often find myself reciting the poems aloud. Once, when I was particularly tired, I remember flopping down on the grass in the outer garden of the Meiji Shrine, opening my copy of *Leaves of Grass*, and reading avidly for the better part of an autumn day. Even now, there are three yellowed gingko leaves from that day pressed between the pages.

This book was the companion of my youth. No, it would be better to say that this book *was* my youth, for everything that is necessary to youth—courage, passion, the future—I found here, along with the poet's prayers.

Pausing to think about the age in which he lived, one realizes that Whitman must have been looked upon as an extremely odd, heretical sort of poet. Yet Ralph Waldo Emerson, the first person who really appreciated his poetry, was moved to write him a letter praising his work as a "sunbeam."[12] I, like others before me, sensed from these poems a primordial sun whose pure rays pierced the dense clouds to shine upon the earth. These poems have warmed me and given me confidence in the mission I pursue today.

It has been more than a hundred years since this collection first appeared. Yet, what Whitman said in the poem "So Long!" still holds true today:

> *Camerado, this is no book,*
> *Who touches this touches a man.*[13]

It is a book I will remember all my life.

—1968

○○ EACH OF US
○○ A POET

On the sea of heaven the waves of cloud arise,
And the moon's ship is seen sailing
To hide in a forest of stars.[14]

THIS *WAKA*-STYLE POEM was written some thirteen hundred years ago. It is included in the *Manyoshu* (Collection of Ten Thousand Leaves), the oldest extant collection of Japanese poems.

Today, we have sent human beings beyond the reaches of Earth's atmosphere; we have stood on the moon's surface. Yet, reading this poem, one has to wonder if people in ancient times didn't sense the presence of the moon and stars more intimately than we do today. Is it possible they lived richer, more expansive lives than we, who for all our material comfort, rarely remember to look up to the sky?

Immersed in material concerns, clamor and bustle, contemporary humanity has been cut off from the vastness of the universe, from the eternal flow of time. We struggle against feelings of isolation and alienation. We seek to slake the heart's thirst by pursuing pleasures, only to find that our cravings have grown that much fiercer.

This separation and estrangement is, in my view, the underlying tragedy of contemporary civilization. Divorced from the cosmos, from nature, from society, and from one another, we have become fractured and fragmented.

Science and technology have given humanity undreamed of power, bringing invaluable benefits to our lives. But this has been accompanied by the tendency to distance ourselves from life, to objectify and reduce everything around us to numbers and things.

Even people become things. War victims are presented as statistics; we are numbed to the unspeakable suffering and grief of individuals.

The poet's eyes discover in each person a unique, irreplaceable humanity. While arrogant intellect seeks to control and manipulate the world, the poetic spirit bows with reverence before its mysteries.

Human beings are each a microcosm. Here on Earth, we live in rhythm with a universe that extends infinitely above us. When resonant harmonies arise between this vast outer cosmos and the inner human cosmos, poetry is born. At one time, perhaps, all people were poets, in intimate dialogue with nature.

In Japan, the *Manyoshu* comprised poems written by people of all classes. And almost half of the poems are by "poet unknown." These poems were not written to leave behind a name.

Poems and songs penned as the heart's unstoppable outpouring take on a life of their own. They transcend the limits of nationality and time as they pass from person to person, from one heart to another.

The poetic spirit can be found in any human endeavor. It may be vibrant in the heart of a scientist engaged in research in the awed pursuit of truth. When the spirit of poetry lives within us, even objects do not appear as mere things; our eyes are trained on an inner spiritual reality. A flower is not just a flower. The moon is no mere clump of matter floating in the skies. Our gaze fixed on a flower or the moon, we intuit the unfathomable bonds that link us to the world.

In this sense, children are poets by nature, by birth. Treasuring and nurturing their poetic hearts, enabling them to grow, will lead adults to fresh discoveries. We do not, after all, exist simply to fulfill our desires. Real happiness is not found in more and more possessions but through a deepening harmony with the world.

The poetic spirit has the power to retune and reconnect a discordant, divided world. True poets stand firm, confronting life's conflicts and complexities. Harm done to anyone, anywhere, causes agony in the poet's heart. A poet offers people words of courage and hope, seeking the perspective—one step deeper, one step higher—that awakens the eternal soul shared by all humanity.

The apartheid system of racial segregation was a grave crime against humanity. In resisting and combating this evil, the keen sword of language played an important role. Oswald Mbuyiseni Mtshali, a South African poet who fought against apartheid with poetry as his weapon, writes:

Poetry reawakens and reinforces our real, innermost strength; our spirituality. It is the force that makes us decent people, people who are filled with empathy for those in need or pain, those suffering from injustice and other wrongs or societal ills.[15]

Nelson Mandela read Mtshali's poems in prison, drawing from them energy to continue his struggles.

The Brazilian poet Thiago de Mello, lauded as the Amazon's protector, also endured oppression at the hands of a military government. On the wall of the cell in which he was imprisoned, he found a poem inscribed by a previous inmate: "It is dark, but I sing because the dawn will come." They were words from one of his own poems.

Amid the chaos and spiritual void that followed Japan's defeat in World War II, I gained untold encouragement, like many young people of my generation, from *Leaves of Grass*. The connection I felt for Whitman, with his overwhelming sense of freedom, struck me like a bolt of lightning.

Now more than ever, we need the thunderous, rousing voice of poetry. We need the poet's impassioned songs of peace, of the shared and mutually supportive existence of all things. We need to reawaken the poetic spirit within us, the youthful, vital energy and wisdom that enable us to live to the fullest. We must all be poets.

An ancient Japanese poet wrote, "Poems arise as ten thousand leaves of language from the seeds of people's hearts." Our planet is scarred and damaged, its life-systems facing possible collapse. We must shade and protect Earth with "leaves of language" arising from the depths of life. Modern civilization will be healthy only when the poetic spirit regains its rightful place.

—2006

GOOD AND EVIL

AN ENEMY
FALLS FROM THE SKY

WHEN I WAS a boy, I loved going to the fairs held on Saturday nights. The main street leading to the east entrance of Kamata Railway Station would be lined with vendors' stalls and stands. In the summer, there were stalls for netting goldfish and stalls selling fireflies, water-balloon yo-yos, and, later in the season, crickets trilling in ornate cages. There were stands for cotton candy, mint candy pipes, Chinese lantern plants, assorted handmade sweets, and baby chicks. The girls all flocked to the stand with coloring books. It was a time of few amusements, and strolling around the night fairs offered children and adults alike an enjoyable time.

In the summer of 1937, I was nine. With a few coins that my mother had given me tightly clutched in my hand, I was wandering from stall to stall, looking at their offerings. The heat of the day had dissipated into the darkening sky, and it was becoming pleasant out. The street leading to the station was packed with a jostling crowd as people came out to walk in the cool evening air and take in the sights. It was a peaceful scene—young and old, men and women, many wearing summer kimonos, making their way in the dim light cast by the lamps hanging in front of the stalls.

At the end of a long row, there was one stand belonging to a tall foreign vendor. He was thin and wore a gray suit. He was the first Westerner I had ever set eyes on.

"What is he selling?" I wondered. I wanted to go up and look, but I was afraid. In those days, unlike today, it was very rare to see a foreigner. I watched him from a short distance away. He was selling Western-style razors. There were fifty or sixty lined up on his stand, and occasionally he would pick up two or three and call out cheerfully to the people walking past. I could hear him saying, in broken Japanese, "*Watashi, Nippon, daisuki desu* (I love Japan)."

For some reason, I found it hard to leave. I wondered if anyone would buy a razor. I stood there watching for some time, but people just walked by without stopping. He didn't make a single sale. It wasn't simply that his stand was in a poor location; the stands nearby were doing well enough. The cold expressions on the faces of those who passed by seemed to say: "What? A down-and-out foreigner? What's he doing here?" People who had been talking and laughing looked startled and suddenly fell silent when they noticed him. Some even glared at him or showed their dislike with angry or disgusted expressions. The razor vendor couldn't have failed to notice all this, but he kept smiling and repeating, "*Watashi, Nippon, daisuki desu.*"

The attitudes of the passersby were probably influenced by the times. In February 1936, there had been an attempted coup in Tokyo, and then the Marco Polo Bridge Incident in July 1937, which marked the beginning of all-out war between Japan and China. At the time, the idea was drummed into Japanese citizens that their nation was an invincible "land of the gods," and they were superior to all other peoples.

We children naturally came to believe that we were very fortunate to be born Japanese; we were glad that we hadn't been born in a foreign country. Our terrifyingly biased education etched racial prejudice into our impressionable young minds.

Of course, the purpose of propagandizing this supposed racial superiority was to justify Japan's invasion and domination of other Asian countries. The rest of the world, however, observed Japan's barbaric treatment of the peoples of Asia and was not about to believe Japan's fine-sounding claim of "liberating" Asia from Western imperialism.

Japan's educational system also taught the Japanese people a view of history and society acceptable only to them, which naturally led them to become estranged and isolated from the perspectives of the international community. False information is dangerous. So is concealing information.

In December 1937, Japanese military forces carried out what came to be known as the Rape of Nanking, but the facts went unreported to the Japanese people, who all cheered the "glorious" military victory and occupation of what was then the Chinese capital. Japanese war correspondents no doubt accompanied the invading forces, but none reported what actually happened. Nor did anyone report the outrage felt by the rest of the world.

We can't see our own backs, nor our own faces. For this,

we need a mirror. The leaders of Japan should have observed themselves in the mirror of their neighbors, the mirror of the world, the mirror of Asia. They should have humbly listened to their neighbors' voices.

During the summer of 1937, I visited that night fair several times, and each time I couldn't resist checking on the tall foreigner's stall. It was always the same. He kept repeating "*Watashi, Nippon, daisuki desu,*" and he never sold a single razor. Sometimes, people gave him a hard time or made fun of him. He only responded to this harassment with a sad smile.

As I look back on the struggles of a foreigner running a stall at the night fair during an era like that, it's clear he must've been in dire straits. I wondered then why everyone was so cold to him. Wasn't he a human being just like us? The way he was treated both angered and saddened me.

That summer was the last time I saw the razor vendor. As the war intensified, the night fair lights gradually began to fade away.

Is a nation that rejects foreigners therefore kind to its own people? No, on the contrary—nationalism regards the nation or race as sacred and sacrifices its citizens as a means for the nation's ends. My eldest brother was drafted in 1937 and, in 1938, two of my other older brothers were called up. At about this time, essential foodstuffs such as rice, sugar, miso, and soy sauce began to be rationed.

The ultranationalistic mood in Japan intensified as the years went by, and English was eventually banned as an "enemy language." At school, my friends talked about how we would have to use Japanese words in baseball instead of the familiar "strike" and "ball" borrowed from English. Even the "HB" mark on pencils, indicating the hardness of the lead, was translated into Japanese, and the Cherry brand of cigarettes was renamed Sakura, the Japanese name for the tree. Jazz and American movies were also banned. The syllables of the musical scale *do-re-mi-fa-sol-la-ti-do* were replaced by the Japanese version, *ha-ni-ho-he-to-i-ro-ha*.

In contrast to Japan, with its ever-narrowing inward focus, the American government was conducting Japanese language training and research on Japan, in the belief that one needed to know one's opponent in order to win.

Recently in Japan, we are once again hearing with increasing frequency phrases that deliberately stress "ethnic pride" and the "superiority of Japanese culture." This may be a reaction to the loss of confidence accompanying the Japanese economic decline. Individuals, too, tend to put on a tough front when they lack self-confidence. They behave arrogantly because they have a strong sense of inferiority.

Why do many Japanese become consumed with national and racial pride? Is it because they have not embraced the kind of universal values that transcend nation and race, such as human rights or those found in the great world religions?

Just before the end of the war, some eight years after I discovered the foreign razor vendor, I was looking up at the night sky from a bomb shelter. I could see a squadron of B-29s illuminated by searchlights. Their giant silver bodies glowed vermilion, reflecting the fires burning below. From the beginning of 1945, B-29 raids had become a regular feature of our lives. The flames with which Japan had burned China and other countries of Asia and the South Pacific had returned to devour Japan.

Those who had a place to go in the countryside had already left Tokyo. The main street leading to Kamata Station was now filled with weather-beaten chests of drawers and other pieces of furniture left by people fleeing to the countryside. It was a sad sight. Any luggage too big to carry away had been abandoned along the street, as if it was a designated disposal site. The pleasant night fairs were no more than a distant dream.

The Kamata neighborhood had been engulfed in a great conflagration, cruel as hell itself, and reduced to ashes. My family had to relocate under government orders, and we were going to stay with one of my aunts in Magome, Tokyo. But just as we finished moving, her house suffered a direct hit from an incendiary bomb during a major air raid on May 24, 1945. We had no choice but to live in a rough shack with a tin roof that we built atop the burned-out site.

One night, the air-raid sirens were wailing, and the radio announced stridently, "A large squadron of B-29s has entered the Imperial capital." We rushed into our bomb shelter. My parents, younger brothers and sister, my cousins, and perhaps some neighbors were all with me.

My four older brothers were all away at the war, and my father was ill. At seventeen, I was forced to think of myself as our family's mainstay. So on that night, I was looking out the entrance of the dugout to see what was going on. The shells from the Japanese antiaircraft guns, aimed at the B-29s, flew through the sky like fireworks. However, they rarely hit anything.

While in the end there was no direct attack on Magome, I nevertheless spent a sleepless night. Just around dawn, about a hundred B-29s flew away majestically, heading into the eastern horizon. Though they were enemy planes, they were a magnificent sight. I watched them until they were tiny dots in the distant sky.

Just then, someone shouted: "Hey! What's that?" Something was falling from the sky. I took a close look: It was a parachute. A plane must have been hit, and an enemy airman was falling from the sky.

The parachute seemed to be coming right at me. I was startled. "He might shoot me!" I thought but couldn't move. I just stood there, watching the trajectory of the falling enemy. It was only a few moments, but it seemed like hours.

The American soldier dropped something. "Maybe it's important secret documents!" I wondered, but I couldn't take my eyes off him. The parachute continued to come straight at me. Then, with tremendous speed, it flew over my head. The whiteness of the soldier's arm sticking out of his short-sleeved shirt reminded me that he was a "white man." He passed by so close that I could see his face. I was astonished at how young he was, almost like a child, an innocent-looking blonde youth who might have been all of twenty years old.

He was completely different from the "barbaric Americans and British" that I had been taught to expect. This was a phrase frequently employed at the time, and when American soldiers or U.S. and British leaders were depicted in magazines, it was as monstrous, savage brutes. The gap between the reality of the young man who had passed not far from me and the images that had been pounded into me was too great, and I was confused.

Could this really be one of those vicious enemy soldiers? Was this a soldier of the American military which, in day after day of indiscriminate bombing, had burned and killed my friends and defenseless young children?

The airman landed in a field some two or three hundred yards away. I was relieved that the danger was over. Somewhere along the way, I noticed that any feelings of hostility I'd had toward him had completely vanished.

After a brief rest, at around seven, I went outside again. I was concerned about the object that the American had dropped. It was a quiet morning, and it seemed as if the air raid of the night before had been only a dream. I looked around for a while, and I found the object: a thick package wrapped in white bandages. I delivered it to the neighborhood police station, and the elderly policeman immediately telephoned someone and made a report. He seemed agitated, tense.

I left the station, and as I walked along, wondering what had become of the young American soldier, I came upon a circle of people talking on the street. They were discussing him. Apparently, as soon as he landed, a group of people ran up to him and began beating him with sticks. Someone also dashed up with a Japanese sword, threatening to kill him. Beaten nearly senseless, he was eventually led away by the military police, blindfolded with his arms tied behind his back. Hear-

ing this, I felt tremendous pity for him. Surely, he hadn't come
to fight this war out of any desire to do so, I thought.

When I got back and told my mother what had happened,
she said: "How awful! His mother must be so worried about
him."

After the war, I learned that a considerable number of
American airmen were shot down over Japan. Sometimes,
they were treated kindly by the Japanese, but in many cases,
though already injured, they were beaten or killed. I heard
of an incident where a person armed with a bamboo spear
lunged at a captive soldier, shouting: "The Americans killed
my son! Let me take a stab at him!" Anyone who dared call for
restraint in such a situation ran the risk of being accused of
treason: "You're sympathizing with the enemy? Are you Japanese?" This was the atmosphere in Japan at the time.

If one tried to be a human being, one was accused of being
a traitor to the nation. If one wanted to be a patriot, one could
not avoid being a traitor to humanity. Even the simple human
act of sympathizing with another was forbidden.

My encounters with the foreign razor vendor and the
downed young American soldier—taking place at the beginning of Japan's war with China and at the end of World War
II—were both sad events for me. I do not know what became
of either man.

More than half a century has passed since then, and the
majority of Japanese have now never experienced war. The
postwar generation does not bear responsibility for causing the war, but they do have a responsibility to oppose the

ultranationalist tendencies and intolerant ideas existing in Japan today that can lead to war. To fail to oppose them, to fail to act, to remain silent, is a passive form of support for such ideas.

A foreigner living in Japan has said:

> It's because I love Japan that I want it to be a country trusted by the world and respected by its neighbors. If it goes on as it is, ignoring human rights, ignoring the facts of history, shutting its ears to the concerns of its neighbors, it will be ridiculed and disregarded by all. I speak out because I am so terribly worried that this might happen.

From a distant memory, I hear the voice of the man in the faded gray suit calling out, *"Watashi, Nippon, daisuki desu."*

—2001

THE SUPREME
JEWEL

BUDDHISM TEACHES that human life is more precious than the entire major world system (the Buddhist view of this galaxy). I firmly believe that human life must be treated as such. Nevertheless, there have been too many incidents recently reported by the mass media that belittle the dignity of life, making us feel depressed and sad.

Recent news (June 1979) of a possible pardon for Sadamichi Hirasawa, convicted in the Teigin massacre case, moves us to reconsider the dignity of life. This incident took place in 1948, shortly after World War II. Since it involved the deaths of twelve bank employees by potassium cyanide and shocked the entire nation, it still remains vividly etched in the memories of my youthful days. This alone makes this news of great interest to me.

I have no intention whatsoever of discussing whether Hirasawa is innocent or guilty. But he has been confined in prison for no less than thirty-one years, twenty-four years since the death penalty was upheld by the Supreme Court in 1955. I

imagine that his life during this long period has been a contin-
uation of indescribable anxiety and despair, waiting in fear of
execution, which might come at any time. According to various records, he has been detained in prison longer than any
other criminal sentenced to the death penalty in the world.
This is absolutely merciless. I thought it was appropriate that
Minister of Justice Yoshimi Furui was seriously considering
whether to pardon the prisoner on the grounds of humanis-
tic considerations. (Unfortunately, the appeal for amnesty was
turned down in December 1980.)[16]

The Hirasawa case, taken together with the Saitagawa case[17]
—which is currently creating a great sensation now that the
Supreme Court has ordered the lower court to review it—
demand that we reevaluate how criminal sentences are meted
out, especially the ultimate sentence of death.

I have long felt that capital punishment should be abolished. It is true that judicial sanctions are unavoidable if we
are to maintain peace and order in society. But I think that in
order for them to be effective, there must at bottom be some
trust in human beings' infinite worth.

Nichiren writes: "Even a heartless villain loves his wife and
children. He too has a portion of the bodhisattva world within
him."[18] As this passage states, any person, no matter how evil,
has deep within the inherent spirit of love and compassion for
others. Without trust in this inherent potential, the law, no
matter how strictly it may be enforced, will ultimately prove
ineffective. The institution of the death penalty has denied all
such human possibilities. I cannot help thinking that it is a
product of human distrust.

Any person, even the worst villain, inherently has the spirit of a bodhisattva, one who aspires to enlightenment, and moreover, the spirit of a Buddha. Regarding this point, the Lotus Sutra, Buddhism's supreme scripture, relates the parable of the Jewel in the Robe: Once upon a time, there lived a man who had a friend who was a rich public servant. One day, the man called on his rich friend, who entertained him with food and wine. He became completely inebriated and fell asleep. The rich friend suddenly had to set out on a journey involving urgent public business. He wanted to give his friend a priceless jewel, which had the mystic power to fulfill any desire, but his friend was fast asleep. Finding no other alternative, he sewed the gem into the hem of his sleeping friend's robe. The man awoke to find his friend gone, totally unaware of the jewel his friend had given him. Before long, he allowed himself to sink into poverty, wandering through many countries and experiencing many hardships. After a long time, he came across his old friend. The rich man, surprised at his friend's condition, told him about the gift he had given him, and the man, who still wore the same robe, learned for the first time that he had possessed the priceless jewel all along.[19]

This is an allegory recounted by Shakyamuni's disciples as they reflect on their ignorance in forgetting to develop the supreme life condition of Buddhahood and being satisfied with the lower states of life.

No one has the right to take human life, which contains the "jewel" of the supreme life condition, Buddhahood. Attempts are made to justify the death penalty by referring to state interests. The state executes condemned criminals as if it had an undisputed right to do so. Because the death penalty stems from this arrogance, I maintain that it is unreasonable.

Let me expand on the parable of the Jewel in the Robe in everyday terms. Take, for example, the human tendency toward arbitrary faultfinding. Parents, seeing their children's small mistakes, yell at them, "You're stupid and hopeless!" Even adults come to hate one another vehemently for trivial reasons. Good friends or neighbors one day, bitter enemies the next. Never questioning the deeper truth of the other person, they emotionally criticize one another. When one calls another bad names, the other returns in kind. Totally unaware of the existence of the "supreme jewel," they exchange harsh words and hurt each other. These emotional collisions take place far more often than one might imagine.

The fact that one cannot see the supreme jewel in another means that one cannot recognize it in oneself. I believe that we all should fix our attention on this point.

Our children or neighbors can in a sense be a mirror that reflects us as we are. Often as not, when we blame someone for some fault, we may be simply seeing in them a reflection of the dark part of our own lives rather than a true picture of the other person.

In Eiji Yoshikawa's *Musashi*, the master swordsman Musashi tells the little boy Iori, as he gazes up at Mount Fuji:

> Instead of wanting to be like this or that, make your-self into a silent, immovable giant. That's what the mountain is. Don't waste your time trying to impress people. If you become the sort of man people can

respect, they'll respect you, without your doing anything.[20]

I know many people of advanced age living with satisfaction and dignity, enjoying a state of life as lofty as Mount Fuji. Their faces, without exception, all shine like the supreme jewel, polished by having weathered all kinds of adversities in the course of life.

—1979

◖◗ A PIECE OF
◖◗ BROKEN MIRROR

I **HAVE A MIRROR. I** always keep it with me. Actually, it's
nothing more than a piece of broken glass about the size of
my palm. The back is covered with little scratches, but that
doesn't prevent it from reflecting whatever is put in front of
it. A piece of broken mirror, somewhat on the thick side, the
kind you could probably find on any trash heap.

It's anything but trash to me. My parents were married in
1915, and my mother, as part of her trousseau, brought along
a mirror stand fitted with a nice mirror. How many times it
must have reflected the face of the young bride, casting back
an image clear and undistorted. Twenty years or so later, however, the mirror somehow or other broke. My eldest brother,
Kiichi, happened to be home at the time, and he and I sorted
over the fragments and picked out two of the larger ones to
set aside as keepsakes.

Not long after that, the war broke out. My four elder
brothers one by one went off to the front, some to fight in
China, others in Southeast Asia. My mother, her four oldest
sons taken away from her, tried not to show her grief; but she

seemed to grow suddenly old. Then the air raids on Tokyo began, and soon they were a daily occurrence. I could hardly bear to look at my mother's face. As though it might somehow help to protect her life, I kept the piece of mirror always with me, sticking it carefully inside my shirt as I dodged my way through the incendiary bombs that fell all around us.

Eventually, when the war ended, we received notification that my eldest brother had been killed in the fighting in Burma. I thought at once of the piece of mirror I knew he must have carried in the breast pocket of his uniform. It was easy to imagine him, during a lull in the fighting, taking it out and looking at his unshaven face, thinking longingly of his mother at home. I know how he must have felt, because I have a piece of the mirror, too, and when I look at it, it brings back memories of my brother.

In the dark, troubled times after Japan's defeat, I left home and moved into lodgings. The room was small, bare, and ugly, but I was too poor to do anything to fix it up. Of course, it had no mirror, but fortunately I had my piece of broken mirror with me. I kept it in a drawer of my desk. Every morning before I went to work, I would take it out and use it to examine my skinny face, shave, and comb my hair, plastering it with pomade to make it stay in place. Once each day, when I held the mirror in my hand, I couldn't help thinking of my mother, even if I hadn't wanted to. Almost unconsciously, I would find myself thinking, "Good morning, Mother!"

Thinking of his mother once a day—I guess it's the best way for a young man to keep from going wrong. Japanese society at that time was in a state of moral and psychological collapse. Fortunately, I managed to avoid falling into the kind of despair and hopelessness that might have led me to do anything self-destructive. I owe it to that battered piece of mirror.

There were times when the mirror told me that the color in my face wasn't good, that I wasn't looking well. With this as a warning, I would use a few extra rice rationing stamps and get two servings when I went to the lunchroom to eat. There were other times when I stared at my reflection in the mirror, noting the sinister way my cheekbones stuck out, and shuddered with disgust. And at still other times, when I happened to be in a good mood, I would smile to myself in the mirror and break into a soft whistle. In a sense, my mother's care and concern were always with me those days, though not in words. The piece of mirror showed me how I was faring day by day and kept me on the right path.

When Toda was nineteen, he made up his mind to leave the little village in Hokkaido where he had been born and come to Tokyo. At that time, his mother gave him an embroidered jacket. As long as he had the jacket, as long as he wore it when he was working, she told him, he would overcome any difficulties he might encounter. It was white with a dark blue pattern, an intricate embroidery stitched with great care, with all his mother's love and devotion. He kept it all his life.

Toda was imprisoned during the latter years of the war, but in 1945, when the war ended, he was finally released and allowed to return to his home. When he discovered that his house had escaped being burned down in the air raids and that the embroidered jacket was still safe, he told his wife that they need have no more worries. Since the jacket had escaped harm, he knew things would be all right from then on.

An old jacket, a broken mirror, both of them capable of conveying a mother's prayers. Such things have a strange power in them that can support and buoy up the human heart when it falters. No doubt many of you will laugh and say, what old-fashioned sentimentality! But to me, there is nothing the least bit old-fashioned about these feelings. The jacket and the mirror, they are the only things that have not gone out of date.

In 1952, when I married, my wife brought along with her a brand-new mirror stand. From that time on, I looked at my face in the new mirror. One day, I came upon my wife with the piece of old mirror in her hand, examining it with a puzzled look. She was probably wondering why anyone would keep such a worthless piece of junk around, one that wouldn't even amuse a child. When I saw that the mirror was likely to end up in the trash basket if I didn't speak up, I told my wife about the history attached to it, of the link it formed with my mother and with the brother who had been killed in the war. She managed to find a neat little box made of paulownia wood and stored the piece of mirror away in it. The mirror is still safe in its box today.

Even an old fountain pen, if it happened to have belonged to some great writer, is looked on with awe and reverence by the people of later times, for they feel that somehow it is capable of revealing the secrets of the great author's masterpieces.

The piece of broken mirror, whenever I look at it, speaks to me about those hard-to-describe days of my youth, my mother's prayers, and my eldest brother's sad fate. It will continue to do so as long as I live.

—1968

◖◗ THE PATH
◖◗ CALLED DIALOGUE

▌HAVE A PHOTOGRAPH THAT stirs the fondest of memories. In it, I am holding the arm of British historian Arnold J. Toynbee as we walk through the bustling London streets. I believe it was taken either right before or after we shared a stimulating discussion over lunch at a local restaurant. The cord of his hearing aid trails down from Toynbee's ear. Though frail with age and suffering from a chronic heart ailment, the eminent scholar continued our dialogue as we made our way. His words, each undoubtedly costing him precious strength, had the import of a final testament to me.

Toynbee was a great human being and a great scholar born in the United Kingdom. Although he was born into one of England's intellectual families, he rejected the Eurocentric view of history. His approach was to abandon all prejudices and preconceived notions about individuals, peoples, and civilizations, and to cultivate sympathy for those ignored and oppressed throughout history. He believed that to attach importance only to dominant cultures was to close one's eyes to half of human history. And he respectfully studied the vanished civilizations of ancient times as well as contemporary societies that had been overshadowed by the modern West, recovering and restoring the voices of those who had suffered.

Toynbee, in *Civilization on Trial*, quoted the Greek poet Aeschylus: "It is through suffering that learning comes." The wisdom gained by ancient peoples as they endured the misery of subjugation by other cultures, he argued, had paved the way for the birth of higher religions. In his view, religion was the human response to the challenge of suffering and the womb that nurtured the growth of new civilizations.

On display on Toynbee's home mantelpiece were a dozen or so framed photographs. In one small frame was a photograph of schoolmates who had died in World War I. The men in the photo were all young, probably not yet thirty. Toynbee had contracted an illness just before the war started and was not sent to the battlefront. Living out his life to the fullest became his duty to his lost schoolmates.

Toynbee said he would never forget the deep anguish of his friends' mothers when they learned of their sons' deaths. My eldest brother, Kiichi, whom I loved dearly, died in war, too, and I will never forget the sight of my mother, shuddering in grief at the news. Toynbee's firm declaration that "War is evil"[21] is also my deepest personal conviction.

During our dialogue, I asked Toynbee what the saddest experience in his life was. His warm, friendly expression immediately stiffened, as if he were trying to mask a profound sorrow. For a moment, I regretted having asked the question.

"That would be when one of my sons chose to commit suicide in the next room," he said. Sunk deep into the sofa, his hands clasped, he was as motionless as a statue.

Toynbee's schoolmates had died in the war, his son had killed himself. The study where Toynbee worked was a place where, enduring these cruel trials of fate, he pondered questions of life and death.

What is human existence? What is the sanctity of life? He sought someone with whom he could discuss these fundamental issues.

His study of history was actually the study of religion, human beings, and life. His earnest intellectual probing transformed his view of history in his later years to one centered not on civilizations but on religion. Declaring that "human beings cannot live without a religion or philosophy,"[22] he insisted that the way for humanity to overcome its present crisis was to discard petty egoism and restore our interaction with the "ultimate spiritual reality."[23]

Our dialogue covered many subjects, but the "ultimate spiritual reality" of which Toynbee spoke was an important point throughout. We arrived at the shared conclusion that the best description of this ultimate reality was a law inherent in universal life. The philosophical quest of Toynbee, a Westerner, had much in common with the Buddhist wisdom of the East.

My dialogues with leading world figures like Toynbee began in rhythm with and evolved alongside the development of the Soka schools.[24] For instance, I met with the Austrian thinker Richard von Coudenhove-Kalergi in 1967, some six months before the opening of the Tokyo Soka Junior and Senior High Schools. My dialogue with Toynbee, meanwhile, commenced the year after the opening of Soka University—starting in 1972 and concluding in 1973. Thus, during the early years of Soka University, I was in fact a student at "Toynbee University." When our dialogue spanning ten days and totaling more than forty hours drew to a close, I asked him what my grade was, and he replied, "I give you an A."

And when I further asked Toynbee if he had any advice to offer me, he replied: "I think it rather impertinent for me to give personal advice to Mr. Ikeda, because I am an academic person and he is a man of action. . . ." He later sent me a message expressing the hope that I would energetically pursue the path of dialogue for the sake of the twenty-first century.

Our exchange took place in the midst of the Cold War between the United States and the Soviet Union, and in a climate of intense hostility between the Soviet Union and China. After my dialogue with Toynbee, I proceeded to visit all three nations in succession. In every country, there were *people*, and I firmly believed that dialogue was the path we should take as human beings to melt the walls of mistrust dividing us. Immediately before my first trip to China (in 1974), Toynbee conveyed great hopes for my visit, expressing his conviction that it would be of major significance for Japan, China, and indeed the world.

Soon after the first Soka University of Japan graduation in the spring of 1975, I began an energetic round of dialogues in France. One of the people I met with was Club of Rome[25] cofounder Aurélio Peccei, introduced to me through Toynbee. I also met with French author André Malraux and French art historian René Huyghe.[26] In the midst of this crowded itinerary, I managed to find the time to fly to London to present Toynbee with a copy of the Japanese version of our dialogue that had just come off the press. Though he was recuperating from an illness, and I could not see him personally, I gave the book to his secretary, along with a certificate conferring on Toynbee the title of honorary professor of Soka University. That autumn, as if he had been waiting for the publication of our dialogue, he died at eighty-six.

Toynbee once said to me, "You will no doubt receive many more honorary doctorates from institutions around the world than I." Strangely enough, I received my first honorary doctorate from Moscow State University, which I visited immediately after delivering the book to him. Since then, I have received 124 such academic honors.[27] I share each and every one of them with the great Toynbee. Our dialogue, *Choose Life*, has been published in twenty-four languages[28] and is read around the globe, transcending barriers of ethnicity and religion. I have thus far engaged in dialogues with major thinkers and world leaders on more than fifteen hundred occasions.

"Dialogue! Dialogue for the sake of the future!"—this is the lifelong mission entrusted to me by Toynbee. This is why I continue to dedicate myself to dialogue to this day.

Dialogue is my very life.

—2002

○ ○ A SINGLE
○ ○ WORD

WHEN I FIRST MET Rosa Parks on the campus of Soka University of America in California (on January 30, 1993), I was struck by her warm, motherly character. "This," I thought, "must be the gentleness that has so charmed everyone." She always had a sweet smile, she was humble, and yet you could see that she was a person of firm conviction.

Widely known as the "mother of the Civil Rights Movement," Parks is a legend. Her story is told in school textbooks not only across the United States but in many other nations. There is almost no one who does not know who she is and what she has done.

In 1993, U.S. historians and academics were polled on whom they regarded as the most influential American women of the twentieth century.[29] Parks was third on a list that was topped by Eleanor Roosevelt. Parks always remained among the common people. She wisely took care not to allow herself to be treated as privileged.

There are times when a single word can change history, when an ordinary day can become eternally remembered.

There are struggles in which a solitary individual becomes a leader who transforms the world. When Parks refused to obey the bus driver's order to give her seat to a white passenger and said the single word *no*, the bell of change tolled triumphantly for the history of African Americans in the United States. This event took place on December 1, 1955, in Montgomery, Alabama, when the forty-two-year-old Parks was returning home after a hard day's work in the tailoring section of a department store.

Parks noticed, after boarding the bus, that the driver was the same unpleasant man who had forced her off a bus some twelve years earlier. On that occasion, the back of the bus had been full, so she had got on at the front—and for that, the driver had forced her off.

Whites in front, African Americans in back. If there weren't enough seats for whites, African Americans had to give up theirs and stand. All types of discrimination designed to make African Americans feel inferior and "keep them in their place" were openly practiced at the time. This bus driver hadn't changed in twelve years. "Y'all better make it light on yourselves and let me have those seats," he now threatened.

"I could not see how standing up was going to 'make it light' for me," Parks writes in her autobiography. "The more we gave in and complied, the worse they treated us."[30]

The tragic history of her fellow African Americans, their blood and tears, was behind this lone woman's refusal to move. Their ancestors had been brought to the United States in slave ships, treated worse than animals—many had suffered and died from this mistreatment. Mothers were whipped before their children's eyes, and parents could only watch in hopeless despair as their children were taken from them and sold. Even after slavery was abolished, African Americans were exploited, captured and lynched, or killed as sport.

"I have experienced many sad events. Many, many," Parks told me. "One African American youth was arrested on the charge of raping a white woman. He was completely innocent, but he was arrested at the age of seventeen. . . . Eventually he was executed; he was only twenty-one."

Parks worked with her husband, Raymond, and others to try to save such victims, but they faced a thick wall of racial oppression. The civil authorities, the laws, the media, and the American people at large all blatantly trampled on others' inalienable rights as if this were perfectly normal and acceptable.

Parks was sick and tired of putting up with her oppressors' bullying. The more she endured, the harsher she was treated.

The bus driver shouted at her, "Aren't you going to stand up?"

"No," she replied.

"Well, I'm going to have you arrested."

"You may do that," Parks calmly responded.[31]

Her refusal to move was an act of compassion for the unborn generations, a cry to put an end to this senseless discrimination.

A police officer arrived on the scene. When he asked her why she wouldn't stand up, she asked in return, "Why do you all push us around?"[32]

This incident set off an explosion of anger among the

African American population in Montgomery, no doubt partly because of the warm regard in which Parks was held. She had long been respected as a cheerful, warm, and intelligent woman. A boycott of the bus service was organized, led by the young activist Martin Luther King Jr., and thirty thousand African Americans who had patronized the buses acted in solidarity. Instead of commuting by bus, they walked, they shared cars. An African American-owned taxi company offered rides at the same fare as the buses.

Retribution was severe. Parks lost her department store job, and she was besieged with threatening telephone calls. The newspapers printed false rumors, and King's home was bombed. But the solidarity was unshaken, and this nonviolent movement pricked the conscience of America and the world. One year later, the Supreme Court declared segregated busing unconstitutional. From that moment, the Civil Rights Movement gained tremendous momentum, surging forward in a great wave toward equal rights for African Americans.

As the saying goes, "Nothing is as powerful as an idea whose time has come."[33] The courage of one woman changed the world as dramatically as a single spark setting ablaze a parched field.

King declared:

> [Parks] was anchored to that seat by the accumu-
> lated indignities of days gone by and the boundless
> aspirations of generations yet unborn. She was a
> victim of both the forces of history and the forces

of destiny. She had been tracked down by the zeit-geist—the spirit of the time.[34]

The time had indeed grown ripe for change. With her stirring refusal to accept oppression, Parks reaped the first fruit of this ripening.

I have been told that, before our meeting, many of those around Parks were wary of Japanese people because of racist remarks made by a number of Japanese politicians. One can imagine that all sorts of movements might have tried to exploit her name for their causes, so she had to be careful. These concerns, I understand, completely evaporated after our visit.

Parks arrived to the strains of "We Shall Overcome" sung by a welcoming chorus. The moment she and I met, we felt a spark of recognition pass between us. I, too, have spent my life working for a cause. Without words, her determination, her tears, and her hopes reverberated in my heart. She said that she had never met anyone with whom she felt so close and at ease on first acquaintance, adding that she felt she had found a new friend.

On that occasion, I invited Parks to visit Japan, and she gladly accepted, flying to Japan in May 1994. This surprised many of those who knew her, since she had never traveled farther than America's immediate neighbors.

During her visit to Soka University of Japan, she wept as she listened to the student chorus. She explained that it reminded her of a young Japanese woman, a survivor of the atomic bomb blast in Hiroshima, whom she had once seen in the United States. "That young woman liked choral singing too," she recalled. Listening to the singing of these young Japanese women, she couldn't stop her tears. Such was the gentleness and sensitivity of Parks, who has always cherished others' feelings.

Mothers are strong. The people are strong. Parks said that it was her mother who raised her to be strong: "My mother taught me self-respect. She always insisted, 'There's no law that people have to suffer.'"

—1994

A NECESSARY EVIL?

"**A**T ANY GIVEN MOMENT in history, precious few voices are heard crying out for justice. But, now more than ever, those voices must rise above the din of violence and hatred."[35]

These are the memorable words of Dr. Joseph Rotblat, who for many years led the Pugwash Conferences on Science and World Affairs, a global organization working for peace and the abolition of nuclear weapons. Rotblat died in August 2005, the month that marked the sixtieth anniversary of the atomic bombings of Hiroshima and Nagasaki, at ninety-six. In the final phase of his life, he consistently voiced his strong sense of foreboding about the chronic lack of progress toward nuclear disarmament and the growing threat of nuclear proliferation.

The startling development of military technology has entirely insulated acts of war from human realities and feelings. In an instant, irreplaceable lives are lost and beloved homelands reduced to ruin. The anguished cries of victims and their families are silenced or ignored. Within this vast system of violence—at the peak of which are poised nuclear weapons—humans are no longer seen as embodiments of life. They are reduced to the status of mere things.

In the face of these severe challenges, there is a spreading sense of powerlessness and despair within the international community, a readiness to dismiss the possibility of nuclear abolition as a mere pipe dream.

Peace is a competition between despair and hope, between disempowerment and committed persistence. To the degree that powerlessness takes root in people's consciousness, there is a greater tendency to resort to force. Powerlessness breeds violence.

But human beings gave birth to these instruments of hellish destruction. It cannot be beyond the power of human wisdom to eliminate them.

The Pugwash Conferences that were Rotblat's base of action were first held in 1957, a year that saw a rapid acceleration in the nuclear arms race that came to engulf the entire planet. On September 8 of the same year, my mentor issued a call for the abolition of nuclear weapons. The day was blessed with the kind of beautiful clear sky that follows a typhoon, as Toda made his declaration at a gathering of some fifty thousand young people in Yokohama:

> Today a global movement calling for a ban on the testing of atomic or nuclear weapons has arisen. It is my wish to go further; I want to expose and remove the claws that lie hidden in the depths of such weapons.... Even if a certain country should conquer the world using nuclear weapons, the people who used

those weapons should be condemned as demons and devils.

Toda chose to denounce nuclear weapons in such harsh, even strident, terms because he was determined to expose their essential nature as absolute evil—an evil that denies and undermines humankind's collective right to live.

Toda's impassioned call issued from a philosophical understanding of life's inner workings: He was warning against the demonic egotism that seeks to bend others to our will. He saw this writ large in the desire of states to possess these weapons of ultimate destruction.

The idea that nuclear weapons function to deter war and are therefore a "necessary evil" is a core impediment to their elimination; it must be challenged and dismantled.

Because Toda saw nuclear weapons as an absolute evil, he could transcend ideology and national interest; he was never confused by the arguments of power politics. Today, half a century later, the language of nuclear deterrence and "limited" nuclear war is again in currency. I am convinced that Toda's cry of the soul, rooted in the deepest dimensions of life, now shines with an even brighter universal brilliance.

If we are to eliminate nuclear weapons, a fundamental transformation of the human spirit is essential. Since the bombings of Hiroshima and Nagasaki more than sixty years ago, the survivors have transformed despair into a sense of mission as they have continued to call out for nuclear abolition. As people living today, it is our shared responsibility—our duty and our right—to act as heirs to this lofty work of inner transformation, to expand and elevate it into a struggle to eliminate war itself.

In 1982, as Cold War tensions mounted, the Soka Gakkai International organized the Nuclear Arms: Threat to Our World exhibition at the U.N. Headquarters in New York. It toured sixteen countries, including the Soviet Union, China, and other nuclear weapons states and was viewed by some 1.2 million visitors. SGI members also participated in the global Abolition 2000 campaign. The purpose of these and other efforts has been to arouse the hearts of people seeking peace.

To further deepen this type of grass-roots solidarity, I would like to call for the creation of a U.N. Decade of Action by the World's People for Nuclear Abolition and for the convening of a World Summit for Nuclear Abolition as soon as possible. Such steps would both reflect and support an emerging international consensus for disarmament.

Needless to say, young people bear the challenges and possibilities of the future. It would therefore be valuable to hold a gathering of youth representatives from around the world prior to the annual U.N. General Assembly, giving world leaders an opportunity to hear the next generation's views. Affording young people such venues and opportunities to act as world citizens is critical to building the long-term foundations for peace.

Crying out in opposition to war and nuclear weapons is neither emotionalism nor self-pity. It is the highest expression of human reason based on an unflinching perception of the dignity of life.

Faced with the horrifying facts of nuclear proliferation, we must call forth the power of hope from within the depths of each individual's life. This is the power that can transform even the most intractable reality.

To emerge from the shadow of nuclear weapons, we need a revolution in the consciousness of countless individuals—a revolution that gives rise to the heartfelt confidence that "there is something I can do." Then, we will finally see a coming together of the world's people and hear their common voice, their cry for an end to this terrible madness of destruction.

—2006

LIFE AND DEATH

⊙⊙ OUR POMEGRANATE
⊙⊙ TREE

THESE DAYS IN JAPAN, the pomegranate is valued more as a decorative yard tree than as a fruit. But I love the faint tartness on my tongue after splitting the fruit open and biting deeply into it.

When I was a boy, we had a pomegranate tree on our spacious property. It had some knobs on its trunk and an abundance of glossy leaves. During the rainy season in early summer, the tree's red-orange blossoms looked lovely against their lustrous green background. It was pure pleasure to see the thick skin of the fruit ripen to a yellowish red. In the autumn, I often climbed the tree and picked its fruit. How I cherish memories of those transparent, pale scarlet seeds.

It happened just before I entered elementary school: I suddenly came down with a high temperature and was laid up with pneumonia. I vividly recall my feverish nightmares and the injections the doctor gave me. When at last I began to show some improvement, my mother told me: "Look at that pomegranate tree. It's supposed to dislike salt, wind, and sandy soil, like what we have around here, but still it blooms and bears fruit every year. You may be weak now, but you're sure to grow strong someday."

Our home was quite close to Tokyo Bay, less than a ten-minute walk away. She was right: The pomegranate's roots had spread deeply and securely, even in such sandy soil.

People can usually remember the fine details and colors from a number of incidents in their lives—as though they were paintings. Generally speaking, such scenes greatly influence the way we live our lives, the way we conduct ourselves. And since I suffered through more than half my youth in a sickly state, those experiences are especially memorable for me.

That questions about life and death never left my mind during my youthful years has, as you may well imagine, some connection with my constant poor health. As I wakened from a nightmare drenched in sweat, I would find myself wondering about such things as, "What happens when a person dies?" Looking back, I see these were the innocent questions of a young schoolboy.

Around the time I entered grade school, I was as mischievous as the other boys. I wasn't very tall, so I was closer to the front of our class lineup than to the end, but I was never daunted in games. My grades were around average. I was just a run-of-the-mill kid without a single characteristic to distinguish me from the others.

I had spent my boyhood days in considerable comfort, but when I was a second grader, my father took to bed with rheumatism and never recovered. Losing the pillar of our seaweed business was a devastating blow to our family. There was no choice but to curtail our activities, which also meant laying off the hired hands.

My mother stood between her husband, who stubbornly refused help from anyone, and her brood of growing children. I imagine her hardships were difficult to bear. My father, forever the diehard, had gotten into the habit of telling us: "If you're a burden to others, you'll have to toady up to them when you mature. Even if you've nothing but salt to lick, don't accept help from anyone!" It was nice in theory, but we were, in fact, destitute. Making every effort to be cheerful, my mother said, "We may be poor, but we're grand champions at being poor."

Somehow, we survived. We never bought thongs for the clogs we wore to school; my mother always braided them for us. An aunt apparently came by from time to time and slipped my mother two or three packages of cigarettes for my father. Kiichi had been anxious to finish middle school, but he quit in order to peddle vegetables. He pulled a cart more than a mile to get his supply. On Sundays, I lent him a hand, pushing his cart from behind. I remember how hard it was to push up hills.

I understand that a relative who had come to inquire after my father's health once left a hundred yen by the bedside. He told Mother, "Mum's the word!" Presumably, my father died without ever knowing. My mother, who had a deep sense of obligation, first told me about it many years later. In fact, it was some two years after I became Soka Gakkai president in 1960. I immediately visited this relative to convey my gratitude. It was embarrassing, for there was a thirty-year gap between the favor and my thanks.

—1975

○○ TO RISK
○○ OUR LIVES

THE FILM *MOURIR D'AIMER* [To die for love] is extremely popular in Japan. Or at least that's what I hear from my younger friends. Unfortunately, I rarely get to the movies these days.

Set against the 1968 May Revolution in France, this movie is said to be based on an actual love affair between a thirty-two-year-old teacher and one of her seventeen-year-old male students. For a time, the lovers in their passionate sincerity succeed in resisting the numerous pressures brought to bear on them, but eventually charges are filed against the teacher in court. Deeply wounded in spirit, she commits suicide.

One plausible reason for the film's popularity among youth in Japan is the profound impression made by the readiness of the hero and heroine to risk everything for the sake of love. At first glance, the young adults of today seem indifferent to such things, scoffing at sentimentality and declaring that risking one's life for any cause at all is mere "nonsense." And yet, deep down, the hearts of Japanese youth have clearly been touched, even by the rather quaint, old-fashioned notion of sacrificing one's life for the sake of love.

The Love Suicides at Amijima and other works of the seventeenth-century Japanese playwright Chikamatsu Monzaemon also deal with the subject of "love suicide." In these works, the unfortunate lovers, caught in a web of social duties and obligations, find that fulfilling their love can be accomplished only by choosing death.

What moves us about these dramas is that the more the lovers are bound and frustrated by social conventions, the more intense their passion becomes, until it culminates in the final outpouring of devotion, and they transcend the fear of death. For us today, who live in a sterile, mechanized society, where so much emphasis is placed upon mere sexual gratification, something in these plays awakens in us a secret feeling of envy and admiration—admiration for the lovers whose passion is so great that they are willing to sacrifice their lives. To be willing to risk death in order to live the kind of life one believes in: This is the key to understanding and realizing to the fullest what it really means to be alive.

I was impressed when I heard a famous Japanese author share how he became a writer. Growing into manhood during World War II, he had fully resigned himself to going off to the front. He was never in terror of dying, but each time the thought of it flashed across his mind, he became more intensely aware of how irreplaceable were the moments of life remaining to him. The memory of these youthful feelings and the desire to understand the true meaning of life, he reported, led him to take up the pursuit of literature.

Before 1945 and the end of the war, many young Japanese men believed that life was something one should be prepared to sacrifice for the sake of one's country. In fact, many of them did, their youthful lives tragically ending on the battlefield. After 1945, however, an intense reaction against such thinking set in, and it came to be regarded as anachronistic to believe that there was anything at all worth risking one's life for. The young people who have no memory of the war seem to be groping restlessly for something to give meaning to their lives in the emptiness of their daily existence. The uneasy feelings of the young manifest themselves in various ways, driving some to reject the entire establishment and its values and adopt alternative lifestyles. For others, the uneasiness erupts as violent resistance to the established order.

A newspaper article I once read about prison inmates brought home to me how an awareness of death can affect one's whole attitude toward life. According to the article, prisoners on death row show an acute sensitivity to their surroundings and are given to almost abnormally intense moods of alternating delight and anger, elation and melancholy. By contrast, the emotional responses of the lifers, it was found, become increasingly feeble until, indifferent to their surroundings, they lose their entire individuality in a generalized posture of servile obedience.

In conclusion, the article compared the psychological malaise of the lifers with the malaise of those "sentenced to life" in our present "managed" society. Certainly, all of us must at one time or another have felt that whatever freedom we have had in modern society has been so circumscribed and "managed" by forces beyond our control that we can no longer enjoy living.

Now and again, however, some individual decides that he can no longer allow his life to be prescribed. On November 25, 1970, we were shocked to learn about the grim suicide of Yukio Mishima, the internationally acclaimed novelist and playwright. Here was a man who had dared to resort to the extreme act of dying for his principles. One could say that, though his last-minute public demands may have sounded irrational, Mishima's pleas constituted a challenge to a society in which people cannot squarely examine issues of life and death.

Surely, anyone who faces imminent death becomes intensely aware of life, since so few moments of it remain. An apt example is the famous novelist Ryunosuke Akutagawa: Before he committed suicide in 1927 at the age of thirty-five, he wrote in his suicide note how beautiful all of nature seemed to him. "Nature is beautiful," he wrote, "because it comes to my eyes in their last extremity."[36]

Personally, however, I feel somewhat unhappy with the implication that it is only through the thought of death that we can become aware of the meaning of life. Must we face imminent demise before we can understand what it means to be alive? This seems to me too shallow and limiting an outlook; it persists in viewing life and death as separate and opposing entities.

In the course of our conversations, pioneer of European integration Richard von Coudenhove-Kalergi and I touched on the widely divergent ways of looking at life and death. He pointed out that people in the East tend to think of life and death as a single page in a book—a page which, when it comes to an end, can be turned, so that one may move on to another page. By contrast, people in the West tend to think of birth, or the beginning of life, as the first page and death as the last page of a book. This trenchantly illustrates these two contrasting ways of looking at life and death.

Life as an endless succession of births and deaths: This is the Eastern view. In this view, we must seek our goal and mission in something that transcends birth and death, something that we are willing to risk our lives for. Only then can we arrive at a true realization of the inexhaustible nature of life. In other words, we must advance beyond the mere struggle to stay alive and be prepared to ask ourselves for what purpose we live.

Each of us must try to discover the particular theme or motif that we believe should characterize our life. An intense seriousness toward each fleeting moment of life, an attitude harboring no regret, regardless of when death may come, can change our whole way of life.

We saw examples of such commitment in this morning's paper, which reported how thousands of young Japanese turned out to demonstrate in support of International Anti-War Day. Once again, youthful energies were expended, youthful hopes were frustrated and dashed against the pavement. These young men and women on the streets of Tokyo in 1971 somehow merged in my mind's eye with pictures I had seen of French youth carrying anti-establishment banners on the streets of Paris in 1968. The faces of those who fell wounded during these demonstrations continue to haunt me.

—1971

◯◯ MY MENTOR'S
◯◯ DEATH

FEBRUARY, the coldest time of the year—the eleventh of this freezing month is Toda's birthday. In my home, we continue to celebrate his birthday, preparing festive red rice with all the trimmings. After all, for me and my wife, Toda will always be our mentor.

April 2 is the anniversary of Toda's death. I cannot possibly forget this day in 1958, which has become a date of permanent significance in my life. Toda, extremely debilitated, had assumed responsibility for a large Buddhist ceremony in Fujinomiya. On April 1, however, he returned to Tokyo and entered the Nihon University Hospital. The evening of April 2, I attended a joint conference of Soka Gakkai executives at our old headquarters.

At 6:45 that evening, I had a phone call from Toda's son, Takahisa, who was at the hospital. I picked up the receiver. Through it came the calm voice, "Father just died." I was thunderstruck. What went through my head at that moment beggars description. What in all the world is more sorrowful than the death of one's mentor? Absolutely nothing . . . for me! He was everything to me—a stern father, an affectionate father.

"Sleep well, Sensei," I said. "You were so weary." The events of the day before his death flashed through my mind like a kaleidoscope: One forty in the morning, prepare to accompany Toda from Fujinomiya to Tokyo. Two o'clock, carried Toda from his lodgings, futon and all. "I'm going along with you, Sensei," I told him. "Good," he said. "My glasses, my glasses." Two twenty, to the car in a stretcher. In the car with his wife and the doctor. Under a dim moon, driving over hushed country roads to Numazu Station.

Arrive in Numazu at three forty-five. Board the express train Izumo due to leave at four fifteen. I'll never forget the smile on Toda's face when I said, "Now, we've got it made!" Six forty-five, arrive at Tokyo Station. Not a wink of sleep. Off to Nihon University Hospital.

And then April 2. . . . Our mentor was dead. The followers he left behind were bereft and perplexed. Whenever we thought of our interminable sorrow, it was certainly natural to feel bewildered about our future. I had pledged myself, however, to carry out his goals into the next epoch.

In February 1958, not long before Toda died, he called me to his home a number of times and told me, "I'd like you to take over after me." Thus, from March 1, 1958, I transferred from Toda's company to work full time for the Soka Gakkai. After that, I had no choice but to assume substantive leadership. A week after Toda's death, I wrote the following poem

on a *shikishi*, a foot-square piece of decorative cardboard used
to record short poems:

> *My mentor has died.*
> *Standing in the vanguard of all*
> *Who spring up from the soil,*
> *I forge ahead*
> *Like a raging wave.*

This *shikishi* hangs permanently in my home.

Looking back, I find that in the eleven years from 1947,
when I first met Toda, until his death, he day in and day out
hammered his discipline into my head. His training was severe
and allowed not a bit of laziness. Had I continued at that pace
for another two or three years, I wonder whether I, too, may
not have done myself in.

Toda often awoke early in the morning and, still in bed,
became deeply engrossed in thought. Once, he phoned me
around four asking me to come right over, and I hurried in
a cab to see him. I suppose he constantly pondered deeply
about his mission.

He loved to drink. Halfway through celebrations like year-
end parties, he often loosened up quite a bit. For example, he
might turn his suitcoat inside out, stick a piece of seaweed
under his nose for a moustache, put his hat on backward, and
do a dance brandishing a broom. Whenever that happened,
we all cheered with glee.

But then, immediately after letting down his hair, he quite

frequently returned to a totally different world. Eyes piercing and unblinking, he became again the stern taskmaster deep in contemplation. There is no doubt that he extended himself to the limit, undergoing extreme hardship and taxing his mind to come up with plans for the future.

The bond of mentor and disciple, based on Buddhist faith, between Toda and his mentor, Makiguchi, was strong enough to last an eternity. I suppose that Toda decided to carry out the last wishes of his mentor and challenge the demonic aspects of government authority the moment he heard from the prosecutor that Makiguchi had died in prison. (The two were imprisoned during World War II for holding firm to their religious convictions in the face of State Shinto.)

In my own case, Toda's death gave me the chance to vow that I might in my own small way realize my mentor's grand dreams. I intend to pursue them steadfastly, dedicating my all to their realization.

—1975

◐◑ THE REAL
◑◐ THING

IN HIS *Essays in Idleness,* Yoshida Kenko writes, "There are
seven types of people one should not have as a friend."[37] He
explains:

> The first is an exalted and high-ranking person. The
> second, somebody young. The third, anyone strong
> and in perfect health. The fourth, a man who loves
> to drink. The fifth, a brave and daring warrior. The
> sixth, a liar. The seventh, an avaricious man.[38]

Kenko started his list with those of a higher social status
and young people. I wonder if I am correct in thinking these
choices are somehow related to his renouncement of the sec-
ular world at the young age of twenty-nine to become a Buddhist monk. I would imagine that his mention of someone
fond of liquor indicates that he himself may have encountered
many drunkards.

Most notable to me, however, is his mention of a strong
person of perfect health. Of course, I do not think Kenko

exactly recommended illness as a virtue. His meaning, as I understand it, was that the inner spiritual depth of a human being can be brought forth by illness, not to mention other difficulties that one experiences in life.

It is true that those who have never experienced being bed-ridden even once are less likely to feel sympathetic toward the weak. But, more than anything else, the suffering of illness is a strong motivating force which, whether one wants to, makes one think about what matters most in life. I am especially sensitive to this point because I myself have had a weak physical constitution since childhood.

Nichiren states, "Illness gives rise to the resolve to attain the way."[39] Those early years when I devoted my entire being to Soka Gakkai activities while keeping this phrase deep within my heart now hold for me fond memories. They are, in Nichiren's words, the priceless "treasures of the heart"[40] that indelibly adorn the pages of my youth.

A masterpiece of Leo Tolstoy called *The Death of Ivan Ilyich* describes the process by which an ordinary human being is gradually awakened to the truth of life, with illness serving as a turning point. In this novella, the author shows unparalleled skill in describing the problem of life and death; its appeal to the reader equals that of any other major literary piece.

The story is about Ivan Ilyich Golovin, an ordinary government official who began his career with the post of confidential clerk and emissary to the governor. He was the son of an official and a member of the elite; he finally rose to a position on the Court of Justice, but the first half of his life was quite simple and ordinary. With his wife and two children, he

THE REAL THING ◀

enjoyed life. His pleasure, as far as his career was concerned, lay in the gratification of his pride; his social pleasure lay in the gratification of his vanity. He also found delight in playing cards. His life as an official continued to go along as he considered it should, pleasantly, predictably; he carried out his job responsibilities tactfully and lived his life as just any other government official.

One day, however, Ivan came down with an ill-defined illness. Having climbed a stepladder to do some drapery work at home, he slipped and fell, hitting his side against the knob of a window frame. The bruise on his side was painful but soon passed. Sometime thereafter, however, he began complaining of a funny taste in his mouth and a sort of lingering uncomfortable feeling in the left area of his stomach. He went to many reputable doctors to find out what was wrong, but none of them could diagnose his condition; his pain steadily grew worse.

Ivan tried to ignore it by concentrating on his job, but the pain in his side would seize him during court proceedings. The story goes on: "It would come and stand directly in front of him and look at him, and he would be dumbstruck, the light would go out in his eyes, and he would again begin asking himself: 'Can it alone be true?'"[41]

Thereafter, Ivan began to desperately carry out his life-or-death struggle against this illness. He said to himself, "This is not a matter of the appendix or the kidney, but of life and death."[42] His honored profession, associations with others, card games, and other pleasures of life that had seemed to fulfill his life now—when compared to the essential question of life and death—felt like a mere illusion. As soon as his struggle with illness began in earnest, whatever had brought him joy from the time of his childhood dwindled before his eyes and became insignificant, often repulsive.

Just two hours before his death, a revelation came to Ivan. The "real thing" came to him. His fear of death vanished and a realization overcame him. Tolstoy puts the finishing touches on his masterpiece:

> "It's finished," said someone standing over him.
> He heard these words and repeated them in his soul.
> "Death is finished," he said to himself. "It is no
>   more."
> He drew in air, stopped at mid-breath, stretched out
>   and died.[43]

Tolstoy's portrayal is true to life.

Nichiren writes:

> The companions with whom we enjoyed composing poems praising the moon on autumn evenings have vanished with the moon behind the shifting clouds. Only their mute images remain in our hearts. Though the moon has set behind the western mountains, we will compose poetry under it again next autumn. But where are our companions who have passed away?[44]

Nichiren talks from the standpoint of Buddhist faith about the transiency of life while conveying the importance of laying a firm foundation every day.

Every phenomenon in life is subject to change and will eventually disappear. Of course, human beings naturally and understandably take delight in the transient aspects of life, but if they consider them to be all that life can mean, they will experience nothing but indescribable emptiness when these phenomena disappear behind thick clouds.

This is just what Ivan realized at the last moment of his life. Our life span is limited. Let us spend each day forging ahead with a seeking spirit, so that we will never lose sight of the "real thing" in life.

—1980

◨◨ AN AGING
◨◨ SOCIETY

JAPANESE SOCIETY STANDS on the cusp of change. Starting from 2007, large numbers of the postwar baby-boom generation reached retirement age—the so-called "2007 problem." The country's over-sixty-five population already stood at 25.6 million, more than 20 percent of the total population, a percentage that will continue to expand. The aging of society is not, of course, something affecting only Japan. According to the United Nations, the global population over sixty—estimated at six hundred million in 2007—will approach two billion by the year 2050.

But the heart of this issue is not in the numbers. The problems of aging presents an opportunity to rethink our social and personal lives in order to ensure the dignity and welfare of each individual. All people have a natural desire to be needed, to have their importance to others tangibly confirmed. Our challenge is to build a society in which people feel valued and fulfilled throughout the course of their lives.

The wisdom and experience of older people is a resource of

inestimable worth. Recognizing and treasuring the contributions of older people is essential to the long-term flourishing of any society. As a country undergoing this demographic shift with exceptional speed, Japan has the opportunity to show a positive example of creatively responding to this challenge.

In a recent survey of members of the baby-boom generation, two-thirds of respondents expressed anxiety about the future. In addition to economic issues, such as the adequacy of pensions and the cost of living, they voiced concern about their health, their ability to care for their parents, etc. Indeed, many caregivers face heartrending daily struggles. There is a clear, weighty responsibility to respond to these voices with sensitive, effective public-policy measures.

The same survey also points to positive attitudes. Although only 15 percent of the members of the baby-boom generation are now engaged in volunteer activities, six in ten said they hoped to be so in the future. And almost eight in ten looked forward to developing deeper relations with their neighbors and community.

I believe that such attitudes—the desire to work for the benefit of others and to strengthen community bonds—can ensure the vitality of an aging society. Individuals who feel needed and strive on behalf of others can keep their youth and energy. They can transform a community, making it a warm, welcoming place to live.

Nichiren writes, "If one lights a fire for others, one will brighten one's own way."[45] Sincere efforts to brighten our surroundings return to illuminate our final years with dignity.

A genuinely happy person is one who has rendered others happy.

I believe that youth can last a lifetime. Inner youthfulness is not a matter of our physical age. Rather, it is determined by the passion with which we live, the enthusiasm with which we learn, the freshness and energy with which we advance toward our chosen goals in life.

Some thirty years ago, I exchanged a series of letters with the well-loved novelist Yasushi Inoue. In one unforgettable passage, inspired by the sight of children setting off to fly kites during the New Year's holidays, he wrote to me, "I feel the need to send something aloft—a kite perhaps—to raise it high into the sky, to let it dance madly in the buffeting winds."

In another letter, Inoue wrote that with age, he found himself increasingly drawn to the "blazing sun," which he equated with a passionate life. The image of striding into such heat, he wrote, symbolized for him the urgent determination to accomplish something—the only proof we are alive.

Inoue was already suffering from cancer and had undergone major surgery when he began writing his final novel, *Confucius.* For the next two years, he continued to work on this novel, which sheds light on the humanity of the Chinese philosopher and his disciples, at times working at a desk brought into his hospital room. I recall him sharing with me, "There is no greater joy than to write one's best work in one's final years, when you are coming to fruition as a person."

Do we view old age as a period of decline ending in death? Or as an ascent toward the attainment of our goals, toward bringing life to a rewarding, satisfying conclusion? A subtle difference in our inner attitude can completely change our experience of these years.

No one, not even those with seemingly limitless amounts of wealth and power, can avoid death. When we become conscious of our finitude, we can earnestly consider the question of how best to live, how to make something truly valuable of our lives. The ideal old age might be likened to a magnificent sunset. Just as the deep red of the setting sun holds the promise of a beautiful tomorrow, a life well lived conveys the gift of hope to future generations.

All of us, not just great novelists, have something we can leave behind. This is the unique, indelible record of our lives, the mark left by our soul on the world. The degree to which we are satisfied with our lives is something only we can judge and be responsible for. And the greatest passages of life are often those written by us in times of struggle.

The ultimate proof of having won in life is to be able to look back with a sense of pride and satisfaction, to be able to say that one lived fully and without regret. Perhaps the most crucial element for an aging society is a spirit of mutual encouragement toward the goal of each of us being able to say, with no hint of hesitation, that this has indeed been a good life.

The challenges of an aging society are not limited to questions of policy. They are an opportunity to reconsider the intimate question of how we choose to live our lives.

—2007

⊙⊙ EVERY MOMENT
⊙⊙ OF EVERY DAY

I **THINK THAT YOUNG** people should have good seniors and conscientious teachers in whatever endeavor they pursue. This invisible human-to-human bond can be defined as the mentor-disciple or teacher-student relationship. In Japan, this relationship is traditionally regarded as the fundamental basis for human growth. Since ancient times, it has been held in higher esteem than the relationship between parent and child or wife and husband.

Yoshida Shoin is one of my favorite persons. A late Edo-period [1603-1868] Confucianist and patriot, he educated a number of young men who were to play a crucial role in the Meiji Restoration.[46] Shoin fostered many men of talent in a short period of time through his private school, called the Shoka Sonjuku, in a remote location in western Japan. He was endowed with exceptional charisma.

Toda often referred to Shoin as an excellent educator, an ideal model who developed many capable people. Even when Shoin was arrested and confined in prison, he wrote many letters to his disciples, encouraging them in whatever way he could to live up to their determination. These letters accurately reveal his character as an educator and a revolutionary.

One of these letters moves me profoundly because it vividly conveys his view of life and death. It was addressed to his disciple Irie Sugizo a half year before Shoin was executed. He calmly states:

> I neither seek death nor do I refuse it. When I am in prison I do whatever I can in prison, and when I am out of prison, I do whatever I can outside of prison. I never discuss the times or situations, and I continue to do whatever I can within my power, until I am destined to go to another fate, whether it be prison or an execution site.

At that time, Shoin was only twenty-nine. Although he was young, when we consider the life he pursued and the depth of his development, we should never mistake this statement as an idealistic aspiration toward death, which can seem characteristic of youth. Rather, what we should read into the letter is his firm view of life and death.

Shortly before his execution, another disciple, Takasugi Shinsaku, asked him, "What is the best place for a man of determination to die?" Shoin gave an impressive answer: "Death is not something to like nor is it something to hate. When one has pursued his course of life to the last moment and achieved peace of mind, then he naturally finds himself having reached the point of death."

Because of his penetrating view of life and death, whatever

Shoin said relating to death never gives us a dark feeling. He had an unshakable confidence in his own actions, and at the same time, he placed his trust in the future and in the human being. In these we see crystallized his true youthfulness.

It is true that this view of life and death has not become popular these days, but that does not mean that the people's concern about death is any less. Rather, people's heightened preoccupation with health and cancer and the like could even be described as abnormal. Isn't there something dark about this?

In stark contrast to the bright light with which Shoin illuminated life and death, people these days are, to the extent they avoid looking at it directly, intimidated by death's shadow. And if a dark fear of death looms too large over them, they will eventually find their life force slipping away.

In a Buddhist scripture, Shakyamuni was once preaching by the Ganges River, when a cowherd in the audience implored the Buddha, with his palms joined together, to accept him as one of his disciples. Shakyamuni told him, first of all, to return to his master with his cows. But the man began to run on his way back, suddenly shouting in a loud voice, "I'm scared, I'm scared!" Some one hundred cattlemen around him each asked him, one after another, "What are you so scared of?" The cowherd said, "I'm afraid of living. I'm afraid of aging. I'm afraid of becoming sick, and I'm afraid of dying." Hearing this, all the cattlemen began to run after him, shouting, "It's dreadful, it's dreadful!" Other cowherds, weeders, firewood gatherers, and onlookers all started running behind them.

This story seems to have no special meaning, but I do not

think we can laugh at the cowherd and the others who followed him so blindly. It is true that the human being naturally fears sickness and death. This is why most of us take good care of our health. To live a healthy life, free of disease, is one of the main factors for a satisfactory life. Having suffered from tuberculosis when young, I was forced to live my adolescence with the fear of death. Therefore, I fully appreciate the value of good health.

On the other hand, we must not forget that living a life free of illness is not everything. If you concentrate too much on your health and neglect other aspects of your life, you will become preoccupied with not having any problems, which isn't a satisfactory way of life either.

A meaningful life results only from having an objective or ideal whose achievement deserves one's lifelong devotion, whose value is everlasting and remains unchanged even after one dies. Buddhism expounds the inseparability of life and death. To live this principle, one has to make every possible effort to live a fulfilling life every moment of every day, because, just as Nichiren says: "This life is like a dream. One cannot be sure that one will live until tomorrow."[47]

We must never allow ourselves to waste our lives. To avert such tragedy, humanity today has to acquire a true understanding of life and death, regarding this as the most important issue.

—1981

CONCLUSION

○○ A REVOLUTION
○○ OPEN TO ALL

IN **2007,** the Doomsday Clock devised by the Chicago-based *Bulletin of the Atomic Scientists* was advanced two minutes, for the first time in five years. It stood at 11:55 p.m., just five minutes away from the "midnight" of human annihilation.[48] This change not only reflected the 2006 nuclear test by North Korea and uncertainties regarding Iran's nuclear development goals, it also reflected the impact of environmental degradation and climate change.

This "clock" was established in 1947, at a time when nuclear weapons were understood to be the greatest threat to human survival. Today, the global ecological crisis casts a stark shadow over the future, one that demands immediate action.

The Club of Rome issued its initial report on the global environment, *The Limits to Growth*, in 1972. Three years later, in 1975, I met with club cofounder Aurélio Peccei. He expressed his deep concern that, unless we change direction, the twenty-first century could see Earth become a barren planet, with both nature and humanity in ruin. Despite the severity of the crisis, he said, leaders in the business, political, and other fields were failing to focus earnestly on the search for solutions; they were more preoccupied with short-term gain, with little thought for future generations. Discussing these realities, Peccei and I concurred that nothing was more crucial than a revolutionary change within human beings themselves.

Humanity has experienced many revolutionary changes over the course of history: revolutions in agriculture, science, and industrial production, as well as numerous political revolutions. But these have all been limited to the external aspects of our individual and collective lives. In other words, while we have made great leaps forward in our technological capacity to control and shape the world around us, we have not achieved a correspondingly dramatic expansion and elevation of the human spirit. As a result, we end up at the mercy of the very forces we have unleashed.

For millennia, humanity has pursued the goal of obtaining the material necessities of our survival. Yet, as Gandhi stated, Earth can produce enough to satisfy everyone's need but not everyone's greed. If our materialistic culture continues to be driven by the unrestrained impulses of desire, it will completely escape our control. Even now, it threatens to consume and exhaust Earth itself, undermining the life systems that support our existence.

Ultimately, all human activities have as their goal the realization of happiness. Why, then, have we ended up producing the opposite result? Could the underlying cause be our failure to correctly understand the true nature of happiness?

The gratification of desire is not happiness. If it were, as Socrates noted, a person who spends his life scratching an itch would have to be considered happy. Genuine happiness can be achieved only when we transform our way of life from the unthinking pursuit of pleasure to one committed to enriching our inner lives, to a focus on *being* more rather than simply *having* more.

Our lives are most effectively enhanced and fulfilled when we seek the kind of happiness that is not limited to ourselves but includes others' welfare. I further believe that a commitment to others' happiness holds the key to peaceful coexistence among people and between people and the natural world.

In the Buddhist tradition, the pursuit of such an ideal is embodied by the bodhisattva. A bodhisattva seeks not simply one's own release from suffering: a bodhisattva is prepared to risk everything in taking action for those who suffer. For the bodhisattva, the interests of self and other are profoundly harmonized; wholehearted efforts on behalf of others are the greatest source of benefit and joy. A bodhisattva is said to fear the loss of the altruistic spirit more than the torments of hell, for to lose altruism is to lose the very reason for one's being.

The Buddhist term *bodhisattva* is not intended to imply the existence of a special kind of person, somehow different or better. Rather, the capacity for altruism is something inherent in every human heart. The term describes anyone—of whatever culture or religion—who acts for others.

Working for people's happiness is something everyone can do, regardless of circumstances. It requires no special titles or qualifications. In the end, it simply comes down to engaging with and encouraging others. But this encouragement is not something offered at arm's length, keeping oneself at a safe distance. Real encouragement is conveyed only in sharing the realities of sufferings and challenges.

Making the effort to live this way amid the corruption of society, striving to offer the gifts of courage and hope, brings out our lives' inner radiance. Encouraging others enables us to fully grasp the meaning of our own lives and experience enduring happiness. The transformation from a self-centered, self-involved way of life to one dedicated to others' well-being is the process of what my mentor called "human revolution."

Even in the face of the severe crises confronting humanity today, I cannot side with the advocates of apocalypse. We can best negotiate the challenges we face when guided by hope, not when motivated by fear.

The inner transformation resulting from even a single person's human revolution holds such hope. This is a revolution open to all, one that does not demand the sacrifice of a single life. When this process achieves a critical momentum— with waves of positive change spreading from one person to another—global society will be dramatically transformed.

This is a revolution that starts here, now—in the heart of every one of us.

—2007

NOTES

Foreword: Deciding for Hope

1. Please go to RAINN (Rape, Abuse & Incest National Network) at https://www.rainn.org/statistics/victims-sexual-violence for the U.S. sexual abuse statistic and UNHCR (The UN Refugee Agency) at http://www.unhcr.org/en-us/figures-at-a-glance.html for the world homeless statistic.
2. The Seventh General Principle is based on an ancient Iroquois philosophy that the decisions we make today should result in a sustainable world seven generations into the future.

Truth Close at Hand

3. Middle schools in Japan at that time were preparatory schools for students aiming to attend one of the Imperial Universities.

Winter Never Lasts

4. Miguel de Cervantes, *Don Quixote*, trans. John Rutherford (New York: Penguin Classics, 2003), 181.
5. Oliver Goldsmith, *The Citizen of the World; Or, Letters from a Chinese Philosopher: Residing in London, to His Friends in the Country* (Glasgow: Printed for J. Steven & Co., Trongate; by Oliver & Boyd, Edinburgh, 1809), 23.

True Friends

6. *The Writings of Nichiren Daishonin*, vol. 1 (Tokyo: Soka Gakkai, 1999), 23.

Children of War

7. National people's schools: In 1941, public elementary schools were renamed national people's schools and took a central role in militaristic wartime education.

Cemetery Days

8. Daisaku Ikeda, *Journey of Life: Selected Poems of Daisaku Ikeda* (New York: I. B. Tauris & Co. Ltd., 2014), 3.

An Unforgettable Book

9. Walt Whitman, *Leaves of Grass* (New York: Bantam Books, 1983), 1.
10. Ibid., 22.
11. Ibid., 41.
12. Ralph Waldo Emerson's quote at http://www.lettersofnote.com/2010/12/i-greet-you-at-beginning-of-great.html.
13. Whitman, *Leaves of Grass*, 401.

Each of Us a Poet

14. *1000 Poems from the Manyoshu*, trans. Japanese Classics Translation Committee (Mineola, NY: Dover Publications, 2005), 52.
15. sgi.org; January 2008 *SGI Quarterly*, 5.

The Supreme Jewel

16. There was much doubt about Sadamichi Hirasawa's guilt, and successive ministers of justice didn't sign the death warrant, so the sentence was never carried out. Hirasawa died in prison in 1987.
17. The Saitagawa case was one of four major cases in the 1980s in which longtime death row inmates won retrials that revealed miscarriages of justice.

18. *The Writings of Nichiren Daishonin*, vol. 1, 358.
19. See *The Lotus Sutra and Its Opening and Closing Sutras*, trans. Burton Watson (Tokyo: Soka Gakkai, 2009), 190.
20. Eiji Yoshikawa, *Musashi*, trans. Charles S. Terry (New York: Kodansha, 1995), 680.

The Path Called Dialogue

21. Arnold Toynbee and Daisaku Ikeda, *Choose Life: A Dialogue*, ed. Richard L. Gage (New York: I. B. Tauris & Co. Ltd., 2011), 7.
22. Ibid., 288.
23. Ibid., 300.
24. The Soka school system, founded by Daisaku Ikeda in 1968, are based on Soka education. The Soka Junior and Senior High Schools—established in Kodaira, Tokyo—were the first institutions to be established. The system now includes kindergartens, elementary, junior and senior high schools, a university in Hachioji, Tokyo, and a university in Aliso Viejo, California. Kindergartens have been established in Hong Kong, Singapore, Malaysia, South Korea, and Brazil.
25. Club of Rome: An organization of individuals, who share a common concern for the future of humanity and strive to make a difference. The Club of Rome's mission is to promote understanding of the global challenges facing humanity and to propose solutions through scientific analysis, communication, and advocacy.
26. Aurélio Peccei and Daisaku Ikeda, *Before It Is Too Late* (London: I.B. Tauris & Co. Ltd., 2009); René Huyghe and Daisaku Ikeda, *Dawn After Dark* (London: I.B. Tauris & Co. Ltd., 2007); André Malraux and Daisaku Ikeda, *Ningen kakumei to ningen no joken* (Changes Within: Human Revolution vs. Human Condition), not published in English.
27. As of December 2016, Mr. Ikeda has received 364 honorary degrees from institutions around the world.
28. *Choose Life: A Dialogue* by Arnold Toynbee and Daisaku Ikeda has been published in twenty-eight languages as of 2017.

A Single Word

29. The survey was conducted by the Siena Research Institution in cooperation with the National Women's Hall of Fame, in Seneca Falls, New York. The findings are based on responses from more than three hundred professors in the fields of history, American studies, and women's studies.

30. Rosa Parks with Jim Haskins, *Rosa Parks: My Story* (New York: Dial Books, 1992), 115.

31. Ibid., 116.

32. Ibid., 117.

33. Commonly attributed to Victor Hugo, this is a paraphrase of his line "An invasion of armies can be resisted; an invasion of ideas cannot be resisted." Victor Hugo, *The History of a Crime*, trans. T.H. Joyce and Arthur Locker (New York: Mondial, 2005), 409.

34. Martin Luther King Jr., *Stride Toward Freedom: The Montgomery Story* (Boston: Beacon Press, 1958), 31.

A Necessary Evil?

35. Joseph Rotblat and Daisaku Ikeda, *A Quest for Global Peace: Rotblat and Ikeda on War, Ethics, and the Nuclear Threat* (New York: I.B. Tauris & Co., Ltd., 2007), 36–37.

To Risk Our Lives

36. Armando Martins Janeira, *Japanese and Western Literature: A Comparative Study* (North Clarendon, VT: Tuttle Publishing, 1970).

The Real Thing

37. Kenko and Chomei, *Essays in Idleness* and *Hojoki*, trans. Meredith McKinney (London: Penguin Books UK, 2013), 117.

38. Ibid.

39. *The Writings of Nichiren Daishonin*, vol. 1, 937.

40. *The Writings of Nichiren Daishonin*, vol. 1, 851.

41. Leo Tolstoy, *The Death of Ivan Ilyich*, trans. Richard Pevear and Larissa Volokhonsky, (New York: Vintage Classics, 2009), 33.

42. Ibid., 30.

43. Ibid., 53.

44. *The Writings of Nichiren Daishonin*, vol. 1, 1027.

An Aging Society

45. *The Writings of Nichiren Daishonin*, vol. 2 (Tokyo: Soka Gakkai, 2006), 1060.

Every Moment of Every Day

46. Meiji Restoration: (1868-1912), a political revolution that brought about the modernization of Japan.

47. *The Writings of Nichiren Daishonin*, vol. 1, 824.

A Revolution Open to All

48. The Doomsday Clock is at 11:57:30 as of January 2017.